THE LION OF POLAND

THE LION OF POLAND

The Story of Paderewski

by RUTH AND PAUL HUME

ILLUSTRATED BY LILI RÉTHI

Hawthorn Books, Inc.   **Publishers**   *New York*

FIRST PRINTING

RL-2038

This is for Michael

AUTHORS' NOTE

Our warmest thanks must go to all those through whose kindness the material for this book was assembled. We are particularly indebted to Mrs. Robert Woods Bliss and to the Honorable Harry S Truman for their generosity of time and spirit in giving us invaluable personal recollections of Paderewski.

The following publishers kindly allowed us the use of copyrighted material: Charles Scribner's Sons, facts and quotations from THE PADEREWSKI MEMOIRS, by Ignace Jan Paderewski and Mary Lawton; Rutgers University Press, a quotation from PADEREWSKI AS I KNEW HIM, by Aniela Strakacz; The Macmillan Company, for facts from PADEREWSKI, THE STORY OF A MODERN IMMORTAL, by Charles Phillips; *Harper's Magazine*, for a quotation from "Paderewski, the Paradox of Europe," by Colonel Edward M. House; the *New York Times Magazine*, for a quotation from "The Paderewski Saga," by Charlotte Kellogg (Mrs. Kellogg is also the author of PADEREWSKI, an excellent biography for young people that would be of special interest to any readers who wish to investigate the subject further); Simon and Schuster, Inc., for the quotation from MEN, WOMEN, AND PIANOS, copyright 1954 by Arthur Loesser; Julian Messner, Inc., for the story of Paderewski's meeting with Clemenceau in 1922 told in THE WORLD OF CARNEGIE HALL, by Richard Schickel.

AUTHORS' NOTE

In an effort to give a complete and accurate picture of Paderewski we investigated every available book and magazine article about him that we could get hold of. The fact that so many *were* available is entirely due to the good offices of the Music Division of the Library of Congress to which we are continually grateful on this and other scores.

RUTH AND PAUL HUME

A Note About Pronunciation

Although Paderewski quickly grew accustomed to hearing himself called "Paderooski" all across America, this is not his name! A Polish "w" is pronounced like an English "v", so he is really "Pa-de-*rev*-skee." Since Polish surnames change their final "i" to "a" when applied to women, his wife is called Madame "Pa-de-*rev*-ska."

CONTENTS

1. A Pounding at the Door 11
2. Debut in Vienna 38
3. The Lion Begins to Roar 57
4. A New World to Conquer 72
5. A Promise Fulfilled 86
6. "They Will Listen" 104
7. The Providential Man 122
8. The Thirteenth Point 134
9. Rebirth of a Nation 147
10. "After That—Art!" 163
    Index 183
    Bibliography 187

CHAPTER 1

A POUNDING AT THE DOOR

The boy lay awake in the darkness, listening.

All evening long the adults in the house had been conversing in agitated whispers, behind closed doors. Now they were asleep—or pretending to be asleep, as he was pretending. The house was unnaturally silent.

Suddenly the boy sat up in bed, clutching the blanket around his shoulders and listening with every ounce of concentration he could muster. His ears were unusually sensitive. Surely he had heard a muted laugh in the blackness outside. Yes—and there was another, and then the sound of low-pitched voices, no longer concealed, and finally footsteps running to the house.

He leaped out of bed and flung open the window. The house was surrounded by Cossacks. Their leader was pounding on the door. "Jan Paderewski!" he was shouting. "Open it up before we break it down!"

The boy could hear the heavy bolt being drawn. By the time he had crept fearfully downstairs it was all over. His father was gone. His sister and his aunt were sobbing in each other's arms. He ran into the courtyard. "Where is my father? What have you done with him?" he asked one of the soldiers. When the man ignored him, he tugged at his coat and cried, "Where are you taking my father?"

A stinging pain shot along his cheek as the Russian whirled and struck at him with a knout. "Let go of my coat, you Polish brat!" the man half snarled and half laughed. He called out some orders to his men, and the troop clattered down the road and out of the boy's sight.

The boy raised his hand to his smarting cheek. The

Cossack rope had ripped across it like a firebrand, and the fire had burned itself into his soul.

Young Ignace Paderewski was only four years old on the night the Russian soldiers took his father to prison for a year. Jan Paderewski had been accused of plotting the overthrow of his Imperial Majesty, Alexander II, Emperor of all the Russias.

What Jan Paderewski had actually done was to allow firearms to be stored in his basement until such time as they might be useful. But besides getting him arrested and imprisoned, they had actually accomplished very little. The revolution of 1863 and 1864 was just one more in a succession of uprisings by which the Polish people struck back at their oppressors. None of these unhappy revolts had ever won back the country's lost freedom, but they kept alive the fierce pride of the Polish people, a pride that the rulers of three nations had tried for nearly a hundred years to extinguish.

Poland, as a nation, no longer existed. The ancient Catholic kingdom had been swallowed up by three hungry neighbors: Germany, Austria, and Russia. It had not, therefore, been swallowed whole, but in

"Where are you taking my father?"

pieces. Three times—in 1772, in 1793, in 1795—the three royal butchers had met over a map of Poland and thought up new ways of dividing the country to their mutual satisfaction. To their distaste they found the Polish people did not agree with their selfish plans.

Ignace Jan Paderewski was born in the Russian third of Poland, on November 6, 1860. His mother died when he was a baby, so his father's imprisonment was a doubly cruel blow. The boy and his older sister, Antonina, were very close. Like all Polish children, they had been brought up on heroic tales of their country's former glory, and their childhood games always centered around the melancholy struggle for freedom. The boy, dressed in a Polish uniform of red and white paper, would charge madly about the house on a hobby horse, smiting his country's enemies with a wooden sword. By the time he was six or seven these games had taken on a reality for him that no one suspected. Young as he was, he determined that when he grew up he would fight for his country, not with a wooden sword but with whatever weapons God would give him. Gradually he took it into his head that only by becoming someone special could he ever hope to help his people and his country to freedom.

Soon after Jan Paderewski's release from prison, he moved his family to the little town of Sudylkow, where the boy grew up. By the time he was three, Ignace's family realized that he had an unusual talent for music. His father, determined to give every possible advantage to his children, brought a music teacher to the house to give them piano lessons. The teacher was a violinist at heart and he could not do much for the children except teach them the names of the notes and set them to playing dreadful duets, arranged from popular operatic arias.

As a student Ignace was rather lazy, but he had a natural gift for languages and a great love for reading the history of his country. When he was ten years old, his sympathetic tutor gave him a book that described the great battle of Grünwald in which the Poles had defeated the greedy German Knights of the Cross and driven them from Poland. As the boy read the stirring account over and over, he was struck by an inspiration. The battle had been fought in 1410. This meant that its five hundredth anniversary was only forty years away—in 1910. "When I grow up," young Ignace promised himself, "I'm going to be rich and famous enough to build a great monument in honor of the anniversary of the battle of Grünwald!"

It was one of those odd fancies that overtake sensitive children. He kept it to himself to avoid unnecessary laughter at his expense.

It seemed obvious to Ignace's father that his son was clearly headed for a career in music. The boy played the piano constantly, although he much preferred to improvise his own melodies rather than practice anyone else's. The music notebook that his proud father had given him was already half filled with random compositions. But how, Jan Paderewski wondered, could the poor boy possibly get the musical training he needed in Sudylkow? When word came to town that a railroad was soon to be built, connecting Sudylkow with Warsaw, the father took it as a sign from heaven. In Warsaw there was a famous conservatory of music. Jan Paderewski swore that his boy would have a chance to study there, no matter how much penny-pinching would have to be done at home in order to finance the venture. In 1872, when Ignace

Ignace and Antonina were very close.

was twelve years old, he and his father set out on the very first train that ran to Warsaw.

It was an exciting and a somewhat frightening adventure. The Warsaw Conservatory did not have dormitories and supervised living for its students, as a modern school would have. The twelve-year-old country boy would be more or less on his own in the big city. Added to this worry was Mr. Paderewski's concern over the fact that his son had had so little formal training in music. Would the entrance exams at the Conservatory be too much for him? As they were ushered into the office of Director Kontski, the father was more unnerved than the boy.

The director looked at Ignace's musical composition book and then he looked squarely at Ignace. The boy returned his gaze without a blink. Kontski turned to the anxious father and said cordially, "We'll take this boy immediately—and without any examinations."

The first hurdle had been taken easily.

Their unexpected luck at the Conservatory had improved Mr. Paderewski's spirits. "Now," he said to Ignace, "all our worries are over! First we buy you a piano! Then we find you a place to live!"

A few hours later his optimism was again on the decline. Although father and son had inspected nearly every piano in Warsaw, they had seen nothing that was not far too expensive. The last address on their list was that of the Kerntopf factory, the most famous piano manufacturers in Poland.

A wasted effort, this one, the elder Paderewski thought gloomily, as he trudged up the stairs to the showroom. If he had not been able to meet the price of lesser piano makers, how could he afford a Kerntopf piano?

Mr. Kerntopf himself greeted the two weary customers. Yes, he told the father, several used pianos were available but they were rather expensive. At the price Mr. Paderewski had mentioned? Well, there was only the old upright over in the corner. The boy was welcome to try it out if he cared to.

Ignace rushed over to the piano and began to play. It wasn't much of a piano, perhaps, but as long as he had something—anything—to practice on, he would be happy.

While he was playing, a younger man came into the showroom and stood listening attentively. After a while he turned to Mr. Paderewski and said, "What plans have you in mind for your son?"

The father said proudly, "My boy has just been

accepted for the Conservatory without an examina-
tion. That's why I want to buy him a piano!''

"Not this old thing!" the young man said. "It
would be worthless in a year. You don't have to buy
him a piano! I will give him one to practice on. For
nothing!"

Mr. Paderewski could hardly believe his ears. He
looked inquiringly at Mr. Kerntopf. "This is my partner and my eldest son," the old gentleman said, shrug-
ging as if to say that there was nothing he could do
about this sort of impulse. But he looked pleased in
spite of himself.

Mr. Paderewski said, "Now I must find a place for
Ignace to live. I would like to get him a room with a
family. He is so young to be alone in the city. Perhaps
you could advise me?"

Edward Kerntopf laughed. "*Here* is a family. It's
a little big already. There are ten children in it, so one
more will hardly be noticed! Leave your boy here and
he can practice on all the pianos in the factory."

Mr. Paderewski beamed. All his problems had been
solved at once.

God works in different ways to help the people

who are close to Him accomplish His work and theirs. In Paderewski's life it happened time and again that when exactly the right person was needed to fill a specific need, that person was always sent to him. Edward Kerntopf was the first of many.

Although young Ignace wept bitterly when it was time to say goodbye to his father, his tears dried quickly. A houseful of youngsters to play with, and a factory full of pianos to play on! It was a splendid combination.

On the day Ignace reported to the Conservatory for his first piano lesson, his excitement was so great that he could hardly walk without reeling. Never in his short life had he looked forward to anything so eagerly. To study piano with a really fine teacher! Young as he was, the boy knew very well that although he could improvise cleverly and could impress his neighbors in Sudylkow, he did not really know how to play the piano correctly. He had a vast natural instinct for music, but such matters as correct hand position, fingering, and proper pedalling were mysteries to him. This was not surprising, since neither of his teachers at home had known much more than he himself knew about piano technique. But now, he thought naively, now at last he would learn everything! Here at the Conservatory some great teacher would give him the key to unlock all the secrets of the piano.

By the end of the first lesson, poor Ignace's enthusiasm had been cruelly dampened. The teacher to whom he had been assigned was a surly type. He listened to the boy play for a few minutes and then said flatly, "You'll never be a pianist. You haven't got the hands for it!" He added helpfully, "I understand you write music. You'd better stick to that!"

It was a blow, but Ignace realized that one man was not the whole faculty. Immediately after the lesson, he went to Director Kontski and asked for another teacher. Unfortunately, the second teacher was exactly the opposite of the first. The first man cared only for ready-made technique and had failed to recognize the boy's natural talent. The second man, with whom Ignace studied for two years, was so poetic and romantic in his approach to music that he paid no attention to the hardcore technical problems of piano playing. Although he had vast admiration for his young pupil, he could not give him what he most needed.

After several discouraging weeks at the Conservatory, Ignace was ready to agree that he was not really cut out to be a pianist. Perhaps he should start thinking seriously about some other instrument. Since he had always liked the sound of the flute, he decided to try it out. The flute teacher decided otherwise. "You'll never be a flute player, boy! You haven't got the lips for it!"

The teacher of oboe and clarinet was a much more agreeable man, but he finally had to admit that Ignace's future did not lie with either instrument. So did the teacher of bassoon and French horn. In time, however, the young musician found his instrumental niche. "Now, my dear boy," the professor of brass instruments told him one day, "you are always trying to play piano. But why? You have no future at all with the piano! Your future is here, playing the trombone!" He flung an arm enthusiastically around Ignace's shoulder. "Don't you know that you are a great natural trombone player?"

The teachers who were most enthusiastic about the

He spent hours at the piano.

new student, however, were the men who taught him theory and harmony and composition. "Never mind which instrument you play best," they told him.

25

"Learn to play all of them because it will be useful to you as a composer. And it is as a composer that you will become famous. As a pianist, never!"

But as he sat night after night in the dimly-lit warehouse, as he worked hour after hour trying to make his fingers produce the kind of sound he wanted to lure out of the piano, he knew that nothing had changed. He would be a pianist no matter who said what. He would be a pianist if it took him a dozen more years to find the right teacher!

Hard work and discouragement did not by any means prevent Ignace from thoroughly enjoying life in Warsaw. For the first time in his life he had a chance to hear real music, properly performed. Edward Kerntopf saw to that. He took the boy to a succession of concerts and operas, and even took him visiting in the homes of Warsaw's leading musicians. Nothing could shake his faith in Ignace's future as a pianist, even though the boy had so far shown progress in nothing but trombone playing.

During his first few days in Warsaw, Edward had taken him to see all the city's beloved monuments to the past. Ignace returned to them again and again, dreaming as he had dreamed from his childhood of the day when his country would be reborn. He liked to walk by the great yellow Zamek, once the royal palace of the kings of Poland. In the palace square stood the noble bronze figure of King Sigismond III, who held a cross in one hand and a sword in the other. Like every other Polish boy, Ignace knew the prophecy that had grown up around the statue: "When Sigismond shakes his sword," the old folks said, "then Poland will be free again!" How many times Ignace went to the square to stare, fascinated, at the statue. Yet the king held his bronze sword rigid and immobile, and it seemed unlikely that he would ever be able to shake it in the name of freedom.

Near the Zamek, in a triangle of fresh green trees, was the shrine of the Mother of Sorrows. The heroic King John Sobieski had built it two hundred years before and dedicated it to "the Queen of Poland." It was here that the boy knelt most often to pray for the liberation of his country and for his own future. Another favorite spot was the seventeenth century Church of the Holy Cross, a spot particularly dear to the people of Warsaw. In its crypt was buried the heart of Chopin, and as young Paderewski saw it for the first time, he must have felt as many Poles had felt before him that the heart of Poland itself was buried in this holy spot. "Where your treasure is," read the inscription over the shrine, "there shall your heart be also."

Although Ignace was a serious boy and a tireless student, he had an incurable streak of mischief in him. In Warsaw, for the first time, he had a real opportunity to exercise it. At home, he had never had any playmates but his older sister, and a boy's older sister is hardly the ideal playmate. But now the rather shy country lad blossomed out and became a favorite among his young fellow students. They called him "Squirrel," in honor of his quick ways and his bright red hair. (Polish squirrels are not gray, but red.) He soon became the ringleader in most of the pranks that went on in the stately corridors of the Conservatory. He also became an expert in the art of playing practical jokes on the older, more dignified students, who frequently called him several names other than "Squirrel."

It was not Ignace's mischief-making, however, that

finally got him into serious trouble with the officials of the school. It was his skill as a trombone player. During the boy's second year as a student, Director Kontski decided to rouse up some publicity for the Conservatory by founding a student orchestra to play at local functions. As the school's finest trombone player, Ignace was naturally drafted into the brass section as first trombone. Final exams were looming ahead. The nearer they came, the more the boy resented the considerable time he had to spend blowing his trombone at rehearsals when he preferred to be studying the complexities of harmony and counterpoint. One day he flatly refused to attend the day's rehearsal.

The outraged director called him into the office and delivered a lecture on student discipline. Ignace countered with some ideas of his own on the useless, time-wasting aspects of the student orchestra. One word led to another, as one word unfortunately does at tense moments. Before he knew exactly what had happened, Master Ignace Paderewski had been expelled from the Warsaw Conservatory.

Fortunately for Ignace, he had friends among the

faculty members. They raised such a fuss in his behalf that the Director was forced to change his mind. The boy was taken back in time to pass his examinations.

A less hot-headed fellow than the red-headed "Squirrel" might have learned a lesson from this extremely close call. But Ignace did not have the sense to stay out of trouble. The next year the orchestra question flared again. Seven students drew up a letter of protest which appeared over their signatures in the newspaper. The seven students were promptly expelled for one year, Ignace among them. This time no amount of influence helped.

Only the loyal support of Edward Kerntopf enabled Ignace to stay on in Warsaw and work at the piano as best he could by himself. And by giving piano lessons to the young children of Kerntopf customers he earned the princely sum of twelve cents an hour.

By the end of the school year he was getting a little bored with this routine and yearned to launch his concert career. So did his best friend, a seventeen-year-old violin student who was also named Ignace. "Why wait around until we're too old to enjoy success?" the seventeen-year-old asked the fifteen-year-old. "Now look, Squirrel. We're wasting our time! The summer vacation is coming. What do people do in summer? They go to summer resorts. And they need entertainment there, don't they? Let's go on tour and present a violin and piano recital. You have enough Liszt and Chopin pieces ready for your half of the program. What do you say?"

"Well—uh—"

"Good! Then it's all settled. We'll tour as far as Russia. That's it! We'll go all the way to St. Petersburg, leaving a trail of triumph behind us!"

Ignace's eyes lit up. "That's it! We'll conquer Russia. We'll show them what a couple of *Polish* musicians can do!"

In the end a cellist joined the troupe, and the foolish trio of young hopefuls started out in the direction of the nearest resort hotel.

"How different from today," Paderewski said later, as he reminisced about his boyhood adventures. "Such a thing could probably not happen in these years of rapid communication, with parents in constant touch with pampered children. Although still youths, we were to a great extent 'on our own,' as you put it, and parental advice was not close at hand. We were completely out of touch with our families. So it was easy for us to keep this great adventure a secret. I knew well enough that my father, had he known, would have no faith in it, nor could he give me any money for such an undertaking."

Whenever the artists reached a new town their first problem was to locate a piano and to persuade the owner to contribute the use of it to the evening's concert. The second problem was to get the piano moved to the hall where the concert was to be played. This was easier, the boys soon found, in a town which housed a military garrison. The good-natured soldiers were always willing to carry the piano in exchange for a glass of vodka. Since every soldier had a different theory about the proper way to move a piano, the entire garrison ended up as an escort. The sight of thirty or forty soldiers surging through the street after a piano, and all arguing at once, was good free advertising. No one in town could long remain unaware of the fact that a concert was to be played that night.

The first few concerts were quite successful and the

three artists moved on, by train, by bus, or on foot, further and further to the north. But as summer faded and the temperature began to drop, the cellist gave notice. "I'm going back to Warsaw," he said, "and if you have any sense, you'll come too."

"Nothing doing!" violinist Ignace replied. "It's on to St. Petersburg for us!"

"Well, I'm not as adventurous as you are. Good-bye!"

Thus the trio became a duo. As the boys turned north and crossed into Russia, they suddenly found themselves in mid-winter. They lined their thin clothing with newspaper and pressed on. They were forced to admit that their brief summer success was over. Soon they were penniless and hungry. Ignace-the-violinist gave in first and wrote home for money. Finally Ignace-the-pianist had to break his resolution and do the same. The fathers of both boys sent money immediately and told the lads to be on the next train home. The violinist was delighted to follow orders. The pianist was more stubborn. "If only I could get to Petersburg. If only I could play one successful concert there!" he thought. "It's just as easy to get home from there as it is from here. Easier in fact. Just one more chance! It's all I ask. Father wouldn't really mind!"

He went on alone to Petersburg. And then real disaster struck. Both his baggage and the money he had counted on for his return home were stolen. He found himself absolutely penniless and half starved in a strange, unfriendly city. Fortunately for Ignace, not everyone in it was unfriendly. A poor plumber took the boy in off the street to save him from freezing to death. With nothing to do all day but try to stay warm, Ignace had plenty of time to think over his foolishness. He had no idea what to do next. On one point, however, he was adamant. He would not write his father again. "How can I?" he said to the friendly plumber. "He already sent me more than he could afford. And I lost it! I can't ask him for more!"

A few days later the janitor of the building came to the plumber's little basement room and said, "Isn't your name Paderewski? There's a letter for you at the General Delivery window of the Post Office."

"For me? But that's impossible. From whom?"

"From a Jan Paderewski. The Post Office has been

asking for you all over town. Just by chance I heard about it."

The letter from home enclosed a hundred rubles. Ignace left Petersburg the next day and was soon safe at home in Sudylkow, thinner but considerably wiser than he had been a year before. One question had haunted him all the way home. "How did you know where to find me?" he asked his father. "And how did you know how desperately I needed that money?"

"Oh, that was easy," Mr. Paderewski said. "You see, I had a dream. I saw you hungry and cold in St. Petersburg, so I sent the letter to the Post Office there and begged them to look for you. The surprising thing is that they found you."

The fact that his father's intense love for him had worked a small miracle on his behalf touched the boy's heart so deeply that he made an immediate resolution. He would repay his father's goodness by doing exactly as his father wanted. He would go back to the Conservatory and finish his studies with no more nonsense. Nor would he put his father to any more years of expense than the good man had originally expected. He was now two years behind his own classmates, but he vowed that somehow he would graduate with them. This gave him six months in which to complete the regular work of two years!

During these months of intensive study, young Ignace began to develop the gift that would carry him through so many crises in his life: an enormous power of concentration.

On graduation day Mr. Paderewski was in the hall, sick at heart because he did not really believe that his son could possibly have passed the rigorous final examinations for the music diploma. As the list of the names was read, as one boy after another went up to the platform, the nervous father braced himself. "But of course his name will not be called. How could it be? The others in the class have been working an extra year and a half . . . There . . . that's the last boy going up now, I think."

But it was not quite the last boy. The last boy was now being called. "And finally," the Director announced, beaming, "with the highest honors of the class, Ignace Jan Paderewski."

Mr. Paderewski remembered few details after that. All twelve Kerntopfs were trying to shake his hand at once, and then Ignace was playing the Grieg Piano Concerto with the orchestra, and everyone in the hall was cheering for him. Then the father realized something that must have made him even happier than this moment of triumph: in six short months young Ignace must have done quite a bit of growing up.

CHAPTER **2**

DEBUT IN VIENNA

Now that Paderewski had his diploma, he determined that he would no longer be an expense to his father. Much as the young man disliked teaching (a dislike from which he never recovered), he knew he had no choice in the matter. If he intended to eat, he would have to teach. But at least he did not have to look very hard for pupils. Immediately after graduation he was offered a position on the faculty of the Conservatory.

Among the students that year was a beautiful young girl named Antonina Korsak. Although Paderewski's future was uncertain, Antonina had complete faith in it. It did not matter in the least to her that at the moment he was only a struggling, poorly-paid piano teacher. In 1880, when Paderwski had just turned twenty, they were married.

He found a small apartment where the two talented young musicians lived in complete happiness and made glowing plans for the future. Paderewski would look back on it as though he were recalling a brief but unforgettable dream. One year after her marriage the beautiful Antonina was dead, leaving her young husband with an infant son.

During her last conscious hours, Antonina, knowing that she was dying, had made her husband promise to take some of her small inheritance and use it to continue his musical studies. Her faith in his future was as bright and untroubled at the moment of her death as it had been during her life.

Now that he had a son to support, Paderewski knew that he must be practical. Nearly everyone who knew anything about it assured him that although he could never make a career as a pianist, he would be a success as a composer. Since no one in Warsaw could teach him any more than he already knew about composition, he decided to go to Berlin to study with a famous teacher named Friederich Kiel. Antonina's mother happily agreed to take care of little Alfred for him.

Professor Kiel was greatly impressed both by Paderewski's talent as a composer and by the young Pole's enormous capacity for work. Too saddened by his wife's death to enjoy the boisterous student life of Berlin, Paderewski devoted himself entirely to his studies. Ten or twelve hours a day of uninterrupted work was not the least unusual.

Although most Berliners were automatically anti-Polish, Paderewski made some good friends among German musicians. His warmest affection was for the great composer, Richard Strauss, whose family accepted the young foreigner as a member from his first appearance in the house. Of all his kindnesses to Paderewski, the greatest favor Strauss ever did for him was a completely unconscious one.

Paderewski knew that he had the habit of making

faces while he played the piano. The more complex the music, the more tortured the grimaces that distorted his handsome face. He had never given the failing much thought, however, until he realized that Strauss had the same bad habit. As he watched the great man play—his face almost as busy as his hands—Paderewski thought, "Good Heavens! That is how I look!" He determined to reform at all costs and did so, but only after months of practicing with a mirror propped up on the music rack of the piano.

Although he did not forget his promise to Antonina to continue his studies, he worried more and more about earning money for his little son. The music he published brought him a great deal of praise but little money. But he soon found a way to increase his earnings. He was in great demand as an accompanist for violinists and singers, since he could sight read music so brilliantly that the performers who hired him did not have to spend much time or money on rehearsals.

One of his closest friends was a violinist named Gorski. He had arranged a short tour of resort hotels, and he asked Paderewski to come with him. The pianist smiled to himself, remembering an earlier tour he had once made. But since this one was on a much sounder financial footing, he gladly agreed to go. There was a marked resemblance, however, in the matter of pianos!

At the very first hotel where they were booked, the piano proved to be of such ancient stock that half the hammers had resigned from active duty. When he struck the keys attached to the afflicted hammer they would fly up, but once up they would not return to place. This meant that each note with a bad hammer could only be used once during the evening.

"I can probably play your accompaniments by faking!" he said to Gorski, "but I can't possibly get through my solos!"

"What can we do? It's the only piano in town."

One of Gorski's young pupils was making the tour with them.

"Excuse me, sir," he said, stepping up timidly. "I think I can help you."

"Impossible!" Paderewski said gruffly.

"Suppose I stand by the piano and push the hammers down just as fast as you hit them. I don't think the audience would notice, do you?"

The two artists looked at each other and shrugged. It was worth a try, since there was nothing else to do. In later years, Paderewski loved to tell this story. "Ah! You should have seen him!" he wrote. "His hands went like lightning. They flew like birds from side to side. He had to lean way across the piano—back and forth he weaved and darted in constant motion. . . What an experience!"

The concert was a huge success. The clever hammer-pusher had been wrong in only one respect: his modest belief that the audience would not notice him. After the concert as Paderewski was walking through the lobby, he heard a man say to his wife, "How did you like that young pianist?"

"Oh, he was all right," came the answer, "but the other one, you know! The second pianist who was playing at the back of the piano! He was the best, I thought. He worked much harder than the other one. He was the real artist!"

Paderewski worked nearly two years in Berlin, interrupted only by a short period of teaching in Warsaw. There, in addition to a heavy teaching program, he began taking private lessons in Latin, mathematics, literature, and history. He did not want his education to be completely one-sided. He had, at the time, no way of realizing how wise a decision this was.

Paderewski's studies in composition had been brilliant, and the piano pieces he published were unusually successful. One of the first pianists to play his work in public was the popular Madame Essipoff. She included his Variations in A minor on many of her programs. To Paderewski, however, Essipoff's greatest attraction was not her success as a pianist but the fact that she was married to the great Theodore Leschetizky.

Leschetizky lived in Vienna, but he was a fellow Pole. He was, in addition, the most famous piano teacher in the world.

The thought of a piano career had remained at the back of Paderewski's mind during every minute of his years in Warsaw and Berlin, although reason told him to abandon the idea. (So had every teacher with whom he had ever studied.) The turning point in his thinking came about quite casually.

One night his publisher invited him to dinner to meet Anton Rubinstein, a brilliant and famous concert pianist. (He occupied much the same position in his day as his namesake, Artur Rubinstein, occupies in ours.)

The famous pianist was charming to the relatively unknown composer and asked to hear some of his piano compositions. When Paderewski had played several pieces, Rubinstein said, "How very fine they are! You must compose more for the piano!"

Paderewski smiled diffidently. "Oh, I can't do too well writing for piano," he said modestly, "because I play so little myself."

Rubinstein's eyebrows lifted. "Nonsense!" he said. "You have an inborn technique. You could have a splendid piano career, if you wanted one. I'm sure of it!"

For a moment the young man was too stunned to mumble a polite reply. It was true that this opinion was only one against many others in the opposite direction. But it was Anton Rubinstein's opinion, and that gave it a few extra votes. In any case it was all that was needed to decide the young man's future. Somehow he would manage the impossible task of raising the money to study the piano seriously. It was

45

his last chance, if indeed it was not already too late, so he could not afford to settle for anything but the best. He would go to Vienna and study with Leschetizky.

Before he could even think about the future, though, he knew that he needed a rest. The years of intensive work, compounded by a constant uneasiness about his little boy's delicate health, had exhausted him. He decided to spend a few weeks in the beautiful Tatra Mountains. There he could think things out— and start adding up figures. What would a few months in Vienna cost? How much did Leschetizky usually charge per lesson? What was the quickest way to raise the money? The last question was a tricky one, since there was no quick way to raise money. It would have to be done piecemeal.

In the village of Zakopane where he stayed, there lived an old doctor who was an expert on the folk music of the region. Paderewski tramped happily through the hills with his new friend, jotting down notes as fast as the good old man could whistle them. One day the doctor said, "Guess who arrived in the village to open up her summer home? Helen Modjeska! Would you like to meet her?"

Paderewski gasped. "Modjeska? Here? Certainly I'd like to meet her!" Who wouldn't? How many times he had cheered himself hoarse over a Modjeska performance in *Hamlet* or *Othello*! Poles all over the world loved Modjeska, not only because she was a great actress, but also because she was dedicated heart and soul to the cause of a free Poland. Since she was one of the most famous actresses in the world, she had done as much as anyone alive to remind the world that there was such a place as Poland.

Modjeska and her husband were delighted with the handsome young musician, and when he played the piano for her the actress was enchanted. "You will have a great career!" she predicted. "You will do great honor to your country. But you must start at once!"

Paderewski smiled. Non-musicians simply did not understand these things! "You are kind, Madame! But I am not ready to start. Not until I have studied much more. And that is not easy to do."

"Studying costs money." She frowned. "I understand that."

He nodded. "I'll raise it somehow. Maybe if I give a few hundred concerts! Next month I'm giving a little recital in Cracow. It might even fill about one

47

quarter of a hall—if the hall is small enough."

The actress's beautiful dark eyes flashed. "Nonsense! The hall will be filled! Sold out! There will not be an empty seat!"

"Thank you, Madame." Paderewski laughed delightedly. "You are very flattering, but I'm afraid the people of Cracow won't quite turn out *en masse* to hear me."

"Perhaps not. Not yet—but they might just turn out to hear *me*. We shall make it a double bill. Paderewski plays, Modjeska recites! What do you say?"

For a moment he was too stunned to say anything at all.

The hall was indeed sold out and the box-office "take" was at least five times greater than the poor pianist had expected. Modjeska's name on the program was the greatest endorsement he could have had in Cracow. People flocked to hear her recite from the beloved Polish poets. They stayed to hear the unknown pianist play his persuasive brand of Chopin. In one evening he had earned enough to live in Vienna for at least three months. The "right person at the right moment" pattern was once more in evidence.

In 1886 Vienna was the heart of the musical world.
The great composer, Johannes Brahms, lived and
worked there. The Vienna Philharmonic was the old-
est and finest symphony orchestra in the world. The
Vienna State Opera was producing its almost flawless
productions under some of the world's finest conductors. Johann Strauss was writing operettas such as
Die Fledermaus and "The Gypsy Baron," while the
whole country waltzed to the "Beautiful Blue Dan-
ube" and "Tales From the Vienna Woods." To the
hopeful young Polish pianist, however, the center of
Vienna's musical life was the studio of Theodore
Leschetizky.

From the phenomenally early age of fifteen, Leschetizky had been recognized as a remarkable teacher,
and while he himself played publicly until he was past
fifty, his greatest gift was the ability to make superb
pianists out of the advanced students who came to him
from all over the world.

When Paderewski called on Leschetizky, the great
man received him cordially. "Of course! You are the

"Play something for me."

young man whose music my wife so admires! Many young composers are kind enough to bring me their new compositions. You have some pieces to play for me?"

Paderewski gulped. Now that he had to put it into words, his mission suddenly looked a bit ridiculous. As clearly as he could, he explained to Leschetizky that he had not come to him as a composer but as a piano student, since he wanted to have a career as a concert pianist.

The older man's bushy eyebrows flew up. "Are you serious? But—how old are you, young man?"

"Twenty-four."

"And at twenty-four you intend to start studying to be a virtuoso? Do you realize what you are saying?"

Although a man is still very young at twenty-four, he is far too old to begin a new career as a pianist. Either he should be well on his way to an established reputation by that age, or he should forget the whole thing. Paderewski knew this as well as anyone.

Leschetizky was now pacing up and down the room nervously. "It is impossible, I tell you! Impossible!"

Paderewski felt as though the world were crumbling into bits and pieces. Seeing the look on his face, the good-natured professor said more kindly, "Well, well—since you are here, play something for me. It does not matter what."

With what desperation Paderewski must have poured into his playing the emotions that were surging through his head at that moment! He played his own compositions, since he knew little else. When he had finished, Leschetizky, who had stopped pacing, said quietly, "You have a great many qualities as a pianist. You have a natural technique, but it lacks so much. Still, you have the principal quality—that is tone." He frowned and shook his head sadly, "But I am afraid there will be too much to do with your fingers. They absolutely lack discipline. Besides," he added, cutting directly to the heart of the problem, "I am afraid you do not know how to work!" This was the thing that Paderewski had known all along. It was, in fact, the reason he had decided he must study with Leschetizky. "If I decide to give you lessons," Leschetizky was saying, "you must start with finger exercises and with Czerny studies." This was where all well-trained beginners started. But it was also the way that every Leschetizky pupil, no matter how advanced, had to begin working towards his lofty goals: absolute mastery of each finger, and a beautiful, singing tone.

Now Paderewski knew how someone feels who must begin learning to walk all over again after a leg injury. As he thumped out his scales and exercises, he realized more clearly than ever how slipshod his playing really was. "I could not improve in a few weeks or months even, because bad habits were already deeply rooted in me, an amateurish way of treating the piano, just play the piano, fingering—anyhow!" No wonder poor Leschetizky almost gave up hope during the early days. "No, no, it's impossible!" he would say, tugging nervously at his beard. "It's too late! It's too late! You have wasted your time on pleasant things like orchestration!" And here he would add the most heart-breaking judgment of all: "Ah, but if you had begun to study earlier. Then you could have become a great pianist!"

But Leschetizky had not reckoned with Paderewski's stubborn determination to work. He practiced seven or eight exhausting hours a day. By the end of each session he felt as though his arms would drop off at the shoulder. There was no time in his life now for anything but work. He who had such a gift for friendship now found that his closest friend was a little spider who ran down a thread and sat on the music rack while he practiced.

In spite of his Spartan existence, Paderewski was completely happy. He knew that he had, at last, found exactly the man he needed. "He opened up another world to me," he wrote later. "After those groping, struggling years, even in a few lessons things became clear. I began to see, to understand, to know how to work. And my thankfulness to Leschetizky is as great today as it was then!"

But life in Vienna was expensive, and although the generous Leschetizky refused to take any money at all for these priceless lessons, Paderewski's small supply of cash finally ran out. Through Leschetizky's influence he was offered a decently paid post at the Strasbourg Conservatory. During that year, he played five important public concerts. The more he played, the more he could see not only how far he had come but how far he still had to go. When the school term was over, he left Strasbourg, determined to get back to Vienna and Leschetizky at all costs. But how?

Once more it was Edward Kerntopf who came to his rescue. He insisted on giving his friend the necessary money. Much as Paderewski hated to impose his problems on anyone else, he felt a strong conviction that some day, in some small way, he would be able to repay Edward's kindness.

And so back to Vienna and Leschetizky, and those driving hours of work. But this time it was different. This time both student and teacher knew that the impossible was actually going to happen.

Before Paderewski had been in Vienna many months, Leschetizky came to his room one day and said, "I have a suggestion to make to you. Would you not like to make your first appearance here in Vienna? Pauline Lucca—she is such a beautiful singer!—is doing a charity concert. She wants to have a pianist on the program too. It's a good opportunity. I think you should take it."

"Yes, I shall be glad to," Paderewski said, his eyes shining. What delighted him to the point of dancing was not the idea of the concert itself. That was just a matter of playing a few pieces during the program so that the singer could rest her voice. What filled his soul with joy was the fact that Leschetizky himself believed he was ready for his debut in Vienna!

CHAPTER **3**

THE LION BEGINS TO ROAR

Nearly all the musicians in Paris came to the piano recital given at the Salle Erard on the evening of March 3, 1889. The French composers Gounod, Massenet, and Saint-Saens were there. So was their famous Russian colleague, Tchaikovsky. It was the sort of audience that is usually described as "small but distinguished." It included many members of the Polish aristocracy in exile who lived in Paris, their "second capital." And they had brought with them whatever friends among the French nobility they could round up for the occasion. It made no difference to them that they had never even heard the name of the young man who was playing. The fact that this Ignace Jan Paderewski was a Polish artist was all they needed to know about him.

From Paderewski's point of view, however, the two most important people in the audience were two Frenchmen named Edouard Colonne and Charles Lamoureux. Both men were conductors of highly successful orchestras bearing their names. And each man was not only constantly on the alert for new talent, but was eager to be first in bringing it before the public.

Paderewski sat in his dressing room before the concert, completely alone, as was his habit. He was not thinking about the audience or anything else in the world except the music he would soon be playing: Beethoven's Thirty-Two Variations in C minor; some Chopin (whose music he loved above any other and which he felt that he, a Pole, could play as Paris had not heard it before), and one of the most brilliant and fiery of the Hungarian Rhapsodies by Liszt.

The manager of the hall had been surprised when the young visitor had asked to have the lights lowered to about half their usual brightness. So was the audience, accustomed as it was to recitals played with the gaslight blazing at full power. But early in his concert career Paderewski had found that a bright light on the keys of the piano made it almost impossible for him to play.

What happened that night in the Salle Erard?

We have a report about it from a man who was himself one of the world's greatest pianists, and no tribute can be held in higher regard than that spoken by one artist about another. Alfred Cortot said of Paderewski's Paris debut, "He appeared with the suddenness of a lightning stroke, making a blurring, an eruption in our hearts. Instead of a pianist, an inspired poet took possession of the keyboard."

The listeners, charmed from the first moment by the romantic appearance of the newcomer, grew more and more enthusiastic with each succeeding piece. But after the last encore—the encores lasted for nearly an hour—the audience was on its feet thundering its approval.

Two men in the audience had better things to do than shout and applaud. The minute the last note had died away, conductors Colonne and Lamoureux leaped to their feet and began a race to the platform. Each man was determined to get there first. Lamoureux, by a masterpiece of broken field running around cheering Polish counts, French dukes, and assorted musicians, won the race. "Monsieur," he puffed, hearing Colonne slide to a stop behind him, "I have the honor to invite you to appear as soloist in three weeks with the Lamoureux Orchestra!"

Lamoureux and other new friends pressed the young pianist to arrange several additional solo recitals at once. "You must strike again while this enthusiasm lasts," they told him. "You must reinforce this first success, or people will quickly forget you." All professional artists are aware of the fickleness of the public. Paderewski knew what good advice his friends were giving him. The night's triumph, therefore, instead of making him happy, plunged him into absolute misery.

Why? Because the modest young man, encouraged to try his luck by his success in Vienna, had come to Paris with exactly one program prepared. And he had just finished playing it! He could have postponed his Paris debut until he had a larger repertoire, but it had never once occurred to him that he would be called upon to play anything in Paris but his one recital. And now!

"It's impossible," he told himself on that triumphant evening of March 3. The first program—the *only* program—had taken him eight months to prepare to his satisfaction. Now he was asked to prepare a second program in three weeks! "It's absolutely impossible! I can't even think about it!"

On the morning of March 4, he said, "Well—maybe I could try—"

On the evening of March 23 he appeared with the Lamoureux Orchestra in the Saint-Saens Piano Concerto in C minor. He played it, said the city's toughest music critic, "in a superb and masterful manner." Critics should be embarrassed, the writer added, to praise Paderewski, because they had been so free and easy in using superlatives to describe other pianists.

As a result, there was now a shortage of new words by which to describe the particular genius of the Polish artist. Another newspaper promptly labelled him "the Lion of Paris."

The faster Paderewski's career gathered speed, the harder he worked, "always struggling for perfection, pushing on and on to that ever-receding faraway peak of attainment," he would write of those days. "All work is like that . . . The summit of the mountain is always farther and farther away." He went back to Vienna and prepared more and more programs, and added concerto after concerto to his growing list. He accepted more and better engagements with bigger and bigger box office receipts to show for them. He toured the French provinces—Lyons . . . Nantes . . . Bordeaux . . . Tours . . . Then on to Antwerp . . . Brussels . . . Liège . . . and Vienna again. And always Paris. After three successful seasons in Paris he felt like a real veteran of the concert stage.

The financial rewards of success were important to him because of Alfred, who was now nine years old. It had been evident from the time he was a year old that the little boy, mentally so alert, was not developing well physically. In those days doctors could do very little to improve or even to diagnose his condition. It would seem that he suffered from a congenital weakness of the spine, and possibly of the heart. "Always in the foreground," his father wrote, "was the menace of his illness, a constantly increasing problem to be met. He had his tutors at this time and he was intelligent and gifted. He had a brilliant, clear mind; he loved music too. It was difficult to take him to concerts, but he often went to recitals at the Salle Erard which we could manage easily and he was very happy to go, and touchingly proud of me at these concerts. It was a great excitement to him, a stimulant to his mind. Poor child, he was completely cut off from everything in life except intellectual things, by his great infirmity."

Father and son were together at last. And Paderewski had accepted the fact that the boy would never walk. In Paris Alfred was cared for in the home of the beautiful Mme. Helena Gorska, a friend who gave great love and kindness to the motherless boy and therefore much peace of mind to his father.

Paderewski's reputation made possible another

long-awaited opportunity. In 1889, a great exhibition
—a sort of World's Fair—was held in Paris. It included
a display of pianos from all over the world. Paderewski arranged to have some Kerntopf pianos, up to then
known only in Poland, shipped to Paris and exhibited.
They won a gold medal (after Paderewski had happily and cleverly used every ounce of influence he had
with every one of the judges). The fact that his pianos
—Polish pianos—had come out so well in international
competition was one of the greatest events in Edward
Kerntopf's life. It would never be possible to repay
Edward's kindness, Paderewski thought, but at least
he had been able to do something. Many people who
reach sudden, dazzling success find it all too easy to
forget the people who helped to bring it about. It was
one of Paderewski's principal characteristics, from his
boyhood to his old age, that he never forgot his friends
at home.

The road had led him from Warsaw to Vienna to
Paris. To continue his conquest of the musical world,
Paderewski now turned to London. As his ship
pitched its way across the Channel, the seasick artist
was in no mood for optimism. The conquest of one

city, he knew, did not guarantee success in another city. London in particular had always maintained a chilly "show me" attitude toward artists who came supplied with flowery reviews from foreign critics. Naturally anyone who arrived in the British capital preceded by rave notices like Paderewski's would be under high suspicion.

It came as a nasty shock to Paderewski to find that his London manager, Daniel Mayer, a beginner in the field, had plastered the city with posters advertising the appearance of the "Lion of Paris." Paderewski, a Pole, knew better than the English Mr. Mayer that Londoners simply did not care for this sort of thing. "You make me sound like an incoming circus," he roared at his overeager manager.

Paderewski's gloomy predictions about his first London appearance turned out to be one hundred percent correct. The night was wet and foggy; the hall was half empty; the audience was chilly. The artist, so sensitive to the emotions of the audience, was appalled. And the reviews were ghastly. "Vulgar," "violent," "much noise and little music," "the clay and the jangle of metal," he read about himself in the London papers. The critics seemed determined to cut the lion down to the size of a small tabby cat.

Today we have our own opinion about the cautious critics who complained so bitterly because Paderewski's playing was "utterly at variance with the traditional methods." In England the "traditional methods" of playing certain unfortunate composers often meant rather spineless, languishing, ladylike performances. Paderewski's intense vitality and virility startled the conservative critics of that Victorian era. It would take some getting used to!

After two slightly more successful London concerts, Paderewski went on a tour of the smaller cities. Poor Mr. Daniel Mayer set out on the road with a heavy heart, for he looked forward to financial disaster. To his horror, Paderewski had firmly insisted that his publicity circulars for the provinces should reprint all his London reviews complete! Mr. Mayer, like every other manager in the business, believed in picking out the best and kindest remarks from reviews and cleverly stringing them together with ". . ." and ". . .," thus giving the impression that all the critics had thought everything was wonderful. Yet Paderew-

The admiring lady was Queen Victoria.

ski had vetoed this simple business procedure for a reason that appalled his poor manager. He said it was dishonest. Dishonest! Who cared about honesty in publicity releases, Mr. Mayer moaned to himself. Results at the box office were what counted! And who had ever heard of a rising concert artist with a conscience. It was a luxury he could not afford.

To Mr. Mayer's vast surprise, Paderewski's honesty turned out to be the best policy, financially as well as morally. The people of the smaller English towns felt —quite correctly—that Londoners looked down on them. For this reason they leaned over backwards to avoid following the lead of the big city in making decisions about anything, even the abilities of an unknown artist. The very fact that the London critics had given him rough treatment was a point in his favor. And the fact that he had circulated all of his reviews, good and bad, piqued their curiosity as nothing else could have done. Curiosity and sympathy are a powerful combination at the box office.

Paderewski finished his tour with the sweet sounds of success ringing in his ears. By the time he returned to London, his complete triumph all over the rest of England had been duly noticed. The lines formed at dawn outside the box office of St. James Hall on the days of his concerts.

His appealing personality and flawless manners quickly made Paderewski a popular figure in London society. He made friends among British statesmen as easily as he did among British musicians. The former gentlemen were surprised at his grasp of so many subjects besides music. And the authority with which this romantic-looking, golden-haired pianist discussed international affairs astounded them. The composer Saint-Saens had, with typical French acumen, already summed up Paderewski's gifts. "Paderewski?" he had said one evening, shortly after the Paris debut. "He is a genius who happens to play the piano!"

It was at this time that the most famous of all Paderewski portraits was made. It was a pencil drawing by the distinguished British artist, Edward Burne-Jones. The picture came into being in a delightful way. As Burne-Jones was walking down the street one day, he passed a young man with a radiant face and a halo of red-gold hair. The artist was so struck by this apparition that he rushed around the block quickly in order to pass it again. Then he rushed back home and announced to the astonished household, "I have just seen an archangel walking on the London pavement!" He grabbed a pencil and rapidly sketched what he could remember of the archangel's appearance.

A few days later Paderewski was brought by a mutual friend to pay a call on Burne-Jones. Much to his surprise he was met by his host not with a polite British greeting, but with an ecstatic cry, "It's my archangel!" Before the astonished visitor could say a word, the artist had seized the unfinished picture and gone to work on it.

A lady who heard him play that year wrote about it this way in her diary: "Went to the green drawing room and heard Monsieur Paderewski play on the piano. He does so quite marvelously, such power and such tender feeling. I really think he is quite equal to Rubinstein. He is young, about 28, with a sort of aureole of red hair standing out."

The admiring lady was Queen Victoria. Another victory had been won in his complete conquest of England.

It was time to move on now and the logical world to be conquered next was the new one. In 1891, the firm of Steinway and Sons in New York offered Paderewski a contract for eighty concerts with a guarantee of $30,000. What young artist could refuse such an offer? On November 3, 1891, Paderewski sailed for New York.

CHAPTER 4

A NEW WORLD TO CONQUER

Carnegie Hall in New York City has been the goal of musicians from all over the world for nearly three quarters of a century. But on November 17, 1891, when the new European artist first played there for an audience that had paid a total of only $500 to hear him, the famous hall was barely six months old.

Paderewski was still slightly numb from his first

impressions of the world he had come to conquer! After a long, rough crossing, his ship had docked late on a rainy night. In those days the first view of New York from the harbor was by no means the thrilling sight it is today. The famous skyline did not yet exist and the unlit waterfront consisted of a few dirty, low-lying buildings.

Almost as depressing as the scenery was Mr. Charles F. Tretbar, the Steinway representative who met him at the dock with this cheering welcome: "Well, Mr. Paderewski, we hear you have had a brilliant success in London and Paris. But let me tell you, you need not expect anything like that here in America. We have heard them all, all the pianists, all the great ones, and our demands are very exacting. We are not easily pleased here! Besides, everyone knows that piano playing is not as well rewarded as singing or violin playing, so don't expect any extraordinary audiences. I've done my best for you, but it won't amount to much!"

Paderewski, his secretary, and his luggage, were then deposited at a dismal hotel in Union Square where the two men spent the night routing battalions of mice and bedbugs. Although they were moved to a good hotel the next day, with the profound apologies of Mr. Steinway himself, the lost night had not helped to put Paderewski in a festive mood for his first concert. Nor had his first look at the schedule of his tour arranged by Mr. Tretbar. To his dismay, he found that he was advertised for six solo recitals and three concerts with orchestra during the first two weeks. Each orchestral concert included two concertos. He would be playing six different concertos within six days.

Paderewski was learning the hard way about the energetic all-out American way of doing things! In Europe, a pianist who played six different concertos in one season, much less one week, would be considered a wonder. Four of the concertos he could easily manage, but the other two, although he had played them once or twice, were not really ready for public performance.

All of these troublesome facts, however, he put out of his mind when he walked out onto the stage of Carnegie Hall for the first time and began to play the Saint-Saens C minor Concerto. It was the same work he had played with the Lamoureux Orchestra in Paris. This time he was accompanied by the Symphony Society of New York City, under its handsome young conductor, Walter Damrosch. The evening closed with his own concerto, which gave the New York critics a chance to judge him as a composer as well as a pianist.

But poor Paderewski had little time after the concert that night to worry about the next day's reviews. Damrosch had scheduled the rehearsal for the next concert at ten o'clock in the morning. And at this second concert he was to play not only the Beethoven "Emperor" Concerto and the Schumann Concerto, but, as a bonus for the audience, the fiendishly difficult Hungarian Fantasia for piano and orchestra by Liszt.

Paderewski went back to his new hotel physically exhausted, as always after a concert, and began practicing for the next day's work. He had not struck more than six chords before there was an agitated knocking at the door. The manager of the hotel stood outside, wringing his hands.

"Mr. Paderewski! Playing the piano at this hour?"

"But I have to practice for my next concert. And

nighttime is the only time I have free!"

"Yes, but Mr. Paderewski, we have so many elderly people living in the hotel. We can't possibly have you practicing the piano at midnight. You can understand that!"

He could understand it, yes, but what could he do about it? Suddenly from the depth of his memory came a clear picture of the Kerntopf factory in Warsaw, with its room after room of inviting pianos. He grabbed his coat and called to his secretary, "Goerlitz! Come on! We're going out!"

"Going out? At this hour? Where to?"

"To the Steinway warehouse!"

The nightwatchman at the Fourteenth Street office was surprised to be roused from his slumbers by a wild-eyed man pounding at the door. "I must have presented a strange appearance," Paderewski recalled. "The watchman, however, opened the room where the pianos were stored, and there, in that cold and gloomy loft, I began practicing. There were no lights except the two candles on the piano. It must have been a strange sight as I think back on it—the empty room, with two fluttering candles and the two men, the night watchman and my secretary, each snoring loudly in his corner as I worked on until morning. That was all I had for inspiration!"

Yet in spite of his fatigue, this concert was a greater success than the first one. The reviews of the debut had been of the sort usually described as "mixed." But after the second concert the *New York Times* headlined its account with the flat statement, "The Success of Ignace Jan Paderewski is Assured."

His success might be assured, but poor Ignace Jan Paderewski himself was in sad shape as he doggedly returned to the Steinway warehouse to practice the arm-wrenching Rubinstein Concerto. How long, he wondered, could he go on at his present pace? No wonder Rubinstein himself had made only one American tour in his life and had said, when begged to return, "May Heaven preserve us from such slavery!"

The third concert, a matinee for which he had practiced a total of seventeen hours, was an unqualified triumph, "the real beginning of my career in America." It was not only the critics who were ecstatic. So was Mr. Tretbar. Three thousand dollars, an unheard-of amount of money for a single concert, was taken in at the box office. By the end of the season, Paderewski's appearance in the same hall would bring in nearly twice that amount.

Mr. Steinway himself, although pleased by the box office receipts, did not really care whether he made money out of these concerts. The Steinway firm had thought of the Paderewski tour as a means of advertising its pianos. And what an inspiration the idea turned out to be! In the mind of the public the name "Steinway" became inextricably linked with the name "Paderewski," and the latter was about to move into the household-word category.

Successful as it undoubtedly was, the first American season was full of trials—some small, one a near tragedy. Mr. Tretbar (who, it should be recorded, later became Paderewski's staunch friend and ally) had indeed had little faith in the success of just one more piano player from Europe. To Paderewski's great annoyance he found that his six solo recitals to be given the week after the three orchestral concerts would not be played in Carnegie Hall, but in a small recital room in Madison Square Garden.

"But why?" he asked. "Why? I've just filled Carnegie Hall for you! Why should I play my recitals in a small place?"

Mr. Tretbar shrugged. A solo piano recital would never fill Carnegie Hall, he said. Besides, it was in the contract that Mr. Paderewski would play where and when he was told to play, and he was being told to play in the small hall of Madison Square Garden!

He played three out of six recitals there. When hundreds of would-be ticket-buyers were turned away, disappointed, from the third one, Mr. Tretbar had nothing whatever to say. Mr. Steinway himself ordered the last three recitals moved to Carnegie Hall.

Paderewski's brilliant concerts shed a special lustre over the new hall which until then had simply been one of several possible places to appear in New York City. But soon a new artist's appearance in Carnegie Hall came to be regarded as the real sign that he had "arrived." It was Paderewski's successes there that

79

established the trend more than any other single factor.

Paderewski left New York with the audiences and critics alike solidly behind him. His New York success was repeated all over the country. Although he was naturally delighted to play before packed houses, the economic aspects of the tour were more and more irritating. He was being paid an average of $375 for each appearance, yet the box office income was running upwards of $3,000! Far more serious was the frightening problem that soon began to plague him. As the strenuous weeks wore on, as solo recitals and orchestral concerts piled up, the strain of playing so often in public began to produce a violent physical reaction in his right arm. Before long he found himself playing in almost constant pain. The actual physical basis of his trouble lay in the action of the Steinway pianos of that day. As Paderewski said, they were "universally recognized as the most marvelous instruments in the world." But they had an action that he found extremely heavy and tiring. It simply took too much pressure to move the keys. After much arguing back and forth he finally persuaded the factory to regulate the action of the seven pianos he was using for the tour.

The relief was immense and the discomfort in his arm, although still present, became bearable. Then one dreadful night in Rochester, as he was playing the opening chords of his recital, he felt an excruciating pain tear through his right arm. (Afterwards, when it was too late, he found out what had happened. The piano used in the Rochester concert had just come back from the factory, where a new and unbriefed workman had carefully changed the action back to its original stiffness.) Yet Paderewski stayed on the platform to play the Beethoven "Appassionata" Sonata, one of the most taxing works in the repertoire. He finished the program in a state of near collapse, then rushed off to find a doctor, and to hear the terrifying truth. He had torn some tendons in his right arm and could no longer move his fourth finger. The doctor said, "The situation is very grave, and there is nothing that I can do for you. Nothing but time will help. You must rest." This was easy advice to give, but how does a pianist rest when he has concerts ahead of him for which tickets have been sold? Paderewski did it by rearranging the fingering in every piece of music on his programs so that he could play with only four of the fingers on his right hand. This is like asking a baseball pitcher to fire a curve ball without using his thumb!

It was not the first time that Paderewski had demonstrated the peculiar iron of his constitution. It was certainly not the last.

At the end of the tour he returned to New York exhausted and discouraged, but relieved that the gruelling months were over. He was met by news that both pleased and horrified him. Mr. Steinway, all smiles, announced that various cities not included in the tour were besieging the office with requests for Paderewski! "Now Paderewski," he said expansively, "you are going to give those extra concerts and we will pay all expenses—everything. Every cent that is taken in will be clear gain for you. That will be our small contribution to reward you for what was, I am sorry to say, badly managed at the beginning of your tour."

Generosity of spirit was a factor that meant a great deal to Paderewski, but although Mr. Steinway's thoughtfulness touched him, he was aghast at the thought of playing more concerts. He was also struck by the sobering thought that since his career had probably been wrecked forever by this tour, he might as well make the most of it. He gave the concerts and made more from the extra ones than he had made out of all the others put together.

Paderewski's bleak conviction that the American tours during which he would play more than fifteen hundred concerts for more than five million people. Only one other person has ever equaled his success at the box office—the beloved soprano, Amelita Galli-Curci. The two artists still stand supreme as the greatest money-makers in the musical history of America.

During those American tours, Paderewski did much more than make music and money. He also made friends in high places—firm, devoted friends who respected him for his great spirit as well as for his fleet fingers. And he captured the imagination and affection of the American public as no other artist has ever done.

How to describe Paderewski's electrifying effect

on the public! Many people have tried. Arthur Loesser, in his fascinating book, MEN, WOMEN AND
PIANOS, does it as well as anyone. He says: "The
most flaming pianistic glory in America's history
broke out when the Steinways first put forth Ignace
Paderewski in the autumn of 1891. He was indeed a
performer of very high ability, an artist of unusual
expressive power; yet that was only one element of
his peculiar appeal. His total personality was just
what, in the American idea, a concert pianist's ought
to be, if one were to marvel at him and respect him
at the same time. His chrysanthemum of pale red hair,
the feminine dreaminess and brooding of his looks
coupled with his aggressive, solid muscularity—all this
was strange and might have seemed ridiculous to Phi-
listines. But the reserve of his bearing, the hypnotic
deliberateness and lordly courtesy of his movements,
were the signs of a profound inner dignity before
which a measure of awe could not fail to be felt. He
seemed, verily, the prince of a foreign realm. No
pianist has ever captured the American imagination
as he did, keeping his hold over it for thirty years. He
became a legend: his mispronounced name drew

farmers from their barns, schoolboys from their baseball, real estate speculators from their offices—all manner of unlikely persons from their dens—into a concert
hall to have a look and a listen at him."

The day would come when Paderewski's hold over
the affection of the American public would mean
more to him—and to his country—than he could even
begin to imagine as he sailed back to Europe at the
end of his first visit to America.

CHAPTER **5**

A PROMISE FULFILLED

The money he had made in America was important to him for one reason: Alfred. At last he was able to afford the kind of country holiday he felt would be best for the boy's health. Father and son spent a few wonderful months together in northern France. To his great joy, both his sister, Antonina, and Edward Kerntopf came from Poland for a visit. Antonina brought with her the love and blessings of their father, Jan Paderewski, who was too ill to travel, but the sister could report at first hand how his great pride in his son had illumined the good man's last years.

While Paderewski gave his sore arm a chance to recuperate, he devoted himself to composing. He began work on an opera called "Manru," a folk story of the gypsies who lived in the Tatra Mountains of which he had such happy memories.

His return to the stage was delayed for over a year, for the injured arm was not responding well to the treatments of the numerous doctors who worked on it. The combination of time and a gifted Parisian masseur finally restored the use of his fourth finger, but it never, he felt, regained its original strength.

It was the last year off he would have for some time. During the next decade his spiraling career would carry him at dizzying speed over thousands of miles on five continents. In America, at least, he quickly found a way around the tyranny of train schedules and hotel reservations. He rented his own private Pullman car. In it, together with his secretary, chef and piano tuner, he traveled all over America. The Pullman car was the home where he lived, ate, slept, and practiced during his tours. Although it cost him the equivalent of twenty-five first class fares, it was well worth it. It was, in fact, the reason why his tours could include so many out-of-the-way places and why so many people had a chance to hear him. But the principal advantage to railroad living was the fact that at last he could practice as loud, as long, and as late as he wished!

This was the golden age of American railroading. What rare, romantic moments were added to its history by the roving pianist! All over the country the same sort of scene repeated itself: a lone Pullman car, sitting at night on a siding—waiting, perhaps, to be coupled to the next express train going through Boston, or Chicago, or San Francisco; railroad workers, and even passing hobos, silently gathered around it listening to the glorious sounds of music that poured out across the almost deserted railyard.

Music was not the only thing that came out of that famous car. The hobo population, with its rapid communication system, soon spread the word that the Paderewski car was always good for a free meal. When Mr. Cooper, the magnificent but temperamental chef, finally put his foot down, Paderewski instructed his secretary to have fifty-cent pieces ready for the men instead of food.

Not everyone would find it possible to live happily in a Pullman car. But Paderewski had a happy combination of physical and mental gifts that made this life seem quite pleasant. He slept without any difficulty, putting worries aside and falling into a sound sleep as soon as he went to bed. His bedtime, to be sure, was rather erratic on concert nights. Whenever he played he worked himself up to such a frenzy of excitement that it took him hours to "unwind." But he had two unfailing methods of relaxation—billiards and bridge. He was fiendishly expert at both.

Paderewski's generosity—whether to whole audiences or to individuals—was boundless. Many railroad companies ran special Paderewski excursion trains from the country into the cities where he was playing. If one of these trains was delayed by bad weather, Paderewski would simply wait for its arrival or would add an extra hour of music at the end of the recital for the benefit of disappointed late-comers.

As for his generosity to individuals—it was the despair of poor Goerlitz, who tried hard to set some limit

Hobos gathered around to listen.

to his employer's open-handedness in money matters!
There was no point at all, Goerlitz knew, in even trying to reason with him if the people asking his help
were Polish. In such cases, he was hopeless. But the
secretary often wished that he would not be quite so
generous about matters that were strictly business.
Like fees! There was that incident in California, for
example . . .

A young engineering student named Herbert
Hoover was working his way through Stanford University by a variety of methods. First he organized a
laundry pick-up and delivery service. Then, with another student for a partner, he opened a lecture and
concert bureau. The amateur managers had not done
well with their last attraction—a speech by William
Jennings Bryan—and they hoped to recoup with their
big spring attraction, Paderewski. But the concert
business is filled with pitfalls for the unwary, as the
young men were about to learn. Paderewski's fee was
high for those days—$2,000. Therefore the price of
the tickets was high—higher than the residents of San
Jose and environs were used to paying. The managers
had also failed to notice that the date selected for their

concert was in Holy Week, which cut down attendance still further. Their Paderewski concert turned out to be an artistic triumph—but a financial disaster. When the last word was in from the box office, the poor impresarios found themselves somewhat short of their expenses. It was a solemn moment.

The two students held a hasty conference. The first obligation, of course, was to pay the artist. The local people to whom they owed money for the rental of the hall, the advertising, the printing, and all the rest, would probably accept i.o.u.'s until they could find a way to pay their debts. Fortunately for the two students, word of this leaked out to Paderewski. He took quite a different view of the situation.

"Add up all the expenses of presenting this concert, down to the last penny," he told the young men. "Then subtract it from the box office receipts. Whatever you have left is enough for me."

"But Mr. Paderewski—that will leave you $400 short of your fee! Let us give you a note and pay it back as soon as—"

"No, no, no." He waved aside the suggestion good-naturedly. "It is enough. After all, if I did not *earn* my fee for you, why should you pay it to me?"

This was the sort of fuzzy remark that nearly drove poor Goerlitz out of his mind.

"I hope that some day there'll be something I can do for you!" young Hoover said, as managers and artist shook hands. But he felt slightly foolish as soon as he said it. It was unlikely that a poor engineering student would ever be able to do anything for the most famous concert artist in the world.

It is possible for a person to be blessed with generosity and yet be a little short on patience. Since Paderewski had both virtues to an amazing degree, he gave his time as easily as he gave his money, and of the two commodities, time is often more valuable. Although it often bored him to the point of stupefaction, he was unfailingly polite about hearing young pianists play. A night in Kansas City was typical. Paderewski had played a tremendous recital before an enormous audience—nearly seventeen thousand people. After the performance, as he greeted his friends and admirers backstage, he recognized a lady whom he knew as a former Leschetizky pupil. Her name was Mrs. White. A serious-looking boy of about twelve or thirteen was standing with her as she waited for the crowd to disperse.

After mutual greetings she came straight to the point. "Mr. Paderewski, this boy is one of my prize pupils. Right now he's working on the Minuet. And he's having some difficulty with the turn." Paderewski smiled. Ah the Minuet! The Paderewski Minuet in G! How many youngsters all over the world were "working" on the Minuet! And most of them were having trouble with the turn.

Paderewski looked at the boy. "Sit down at the piano, young man!" he said sternly, his eyes twinkling.

("He scared me half to death!" the student, glancing back over that evening from a vantage point of sixty years, would say.)

The boy sat down and played the Minuet. When he got to the problematic turn, the composer stopped him and gave him careful instructions in the exact fingering necessary to bring it off properly. When the master-class was over, he shook hands and wished the lad success in his musical career. The boy went home in a glow of inspiration and for days worked at the piano even harder than usual. (He was already in the habit of getting up at 5 A.M. in order to practice two hours before going to school.) A few years later, however, the eager young piano student suddenly decided that piano playing was not for big boys. He gave

Paderewski married Mme. Gorska.

up his idea of a career in music and went on to other things, including the White House. His name was Harry S Truman.

On the night of their meeting, of course, neither Paderewski nor the boy had any way of knowing that on a night in Kansas City the future President of Poland had just given a piano lesson to the future President of the United States.

It was not until the year 1899, with a widespread reputation firmly established, that Paderewski accepted an invitation to play a series of concerts in Russia. He had not been back there since the youthful venture twenty years earlier, from which his father's dream had so literally rescued him. On the way to Russia, he played three concerts in Warsaw, returning to his boyhood home where he was received with every kind of honor. It was not so when he arrived in Russia. While audiences everywhere were enthusiastic, Paderewski felt keenly the strong hostility of the conservatories of both Moscow and St. Petersburg.

The real problem lay in the hatred many Russians held for anything Polish. As a Pole, Paderewski felt many slights, heard many unfriendly remarks and even open hissing during his tour. He was not sorry when it was over.

Soon after his return from Russia, Paderewski married the beautiful Mme. Gorska with whom he had fallen in love during the years that she had done her best to act as a mother for Alfred. With his son and his new wife he settled down for a rest on the beautiful estate, Riond-Bosson, on Lake Geneva in Switzerland. He had bought the villa so that Alfred could have the quiet, open-air surroundings prescribed for him. Paderewski was happier than he had been for years.

Riond-Bosson also gave Mme. Paderewska an opportunity to indulge one of her favorite hobbies: poultry farming. The chicken houses as well as the fruit trees of the place became famous.

The grapes of Riond-Bosson were of surpassing sweetness and juiciness. One of their greatest admirers in later years was Paderewski's devoted friend, Achille Ratti, the papal nuncio in Poland. Paderewski always made it a point to supply him with the first growth of these luscious grapes. Even when the papal diplomat took up permanent residence in Rome and could no longer visit at Riond-Bosson, he received his grapes. Border officials sometimes balked at passing the fruit through the customs, but what could a mere customs officer do when told that the grapes were a gift from the beloved Paderewski to his friend, Pope Pius XI.

And when Paderewski went on tour, his wife was his constant companion, remaining in the dressing room while he played and doing everything in her power to shield him from the prickly harassments of concert work.

The great happiness that came to him at his marriage was followed very shortly by a great but not unexpected sorrow. Paderewski, while playing in Spain, was called home by the news that Alfred had died. A lifetime of care, of watchful attention and special treatments had not been able to save him. At twenty, he was buried in the Cemetery of Montmorency in Paris, near the tomb of Chopin.

For Paderewski, work had always been the surest antidote for grief. He now turned all of his energy to the finishing details of his opera, "Manru," which was to be produced at the Dresden Opera in May, 1901.

Eight years of work lay behind the premiere of "Manru," which was shortly thereafter performed in many of the leading opera houses of Europe. The following winter the Metropolitan Opera in New York presented it with an all-star cast and included it in five cities of its annual tour. While the opera had, generally, a friendly reception, one critic remarked sourly, "What a pity that Paderewski is now composing, for he is no more a great pianist." He stood firmly alone in his opinion.

Paderewski had been the favorite pianist of Europe and North and South America long enough for the news of his greatness to spread clear around the world. In the spring of 1904 he set out on a tour of Australia. On this trip Paderewski's baggage problem was complicated beyond memory. The Paderewski menage was enlarged by the addition of some forty parrots. Mme. Paderewska had a fondness for all types of birds, and the talking variety fascinated her.

One of these animals became a special favorite of Paderewski's. Named Cockey Roberts, he was, according to his master, "more than a parrot. He was a real artist in his way." Paderewski's particular delight was Cockey Roberts' habit of perching on his foot during practice sessions. "He would sit perfectly still," Paderewski recalled, "and then from time to time, he would say in a very loving and scratchy voice, 'Oh Lord, how beautiful!' It was touching."

Very few pianists ever retire from public performance, even briefly, at the height of their careers. Paderewski, however, did so in 1906. From causes he describes as partly physical and partly psychological, he had begun to feel a curious but very real aversion to the piano. Not even the estate in Switzerland, where he could let the sometimes healing forces of farming work on his nerves, helped much. When, in order to earn some money, he returned to concerts for a time, he found the distaste for the piano still strong. Physicians tried their arts on him, one even resorting to hypnosis. By 1909 Paderewski said, "The easiest pieces in my repertoire I could not manage. The touch was strange to me. It was torture." Perhaps Paderewski's sudden distaste for his lifelong routine came about because he was beginning to prepare himself subconsciously for a new and wholly unexpected career.

In 1910 an event occurred that was both important in itself and of great significance for the future. 1910 was a year of doubly historic moment in the history of Poland. It was the centenary of the birth of Chopin. It was also the 500th anniversary of the Battle of Grünwald, in which a victorious Polish army had driven out a foreign invader. Paderewski had never once during the past forty years forgotten that a small boy of ten had vowed to build a great memorial in honor of that battle for Polish freedom.

He had commissioned a talented Polish sculptor to design such a monument, and on the 500th anniversary of the battle it was unveiled and presented to the city of Cracow. On the base of it were carved these words:

"For the glory of our ancestors and
the encouragement of our brothers."

As the donor of the new monument, Paderewski made a presentation speech which was marked with the deepest patriotic fervor. Though he spoke quietly, the Cracow speech strongly showed Paderewski's deep knowledge of political affairs. And at a reception in his honor, after the formal presentation, the voice of the pianist was heard in a piece of peculiarly accurate political prophecy:

"Brothers, the hour of our freedom is about to strike. Within five years a fratricidal war will soak with blood the whole earth. Prepare, compatriots mine, brother Poles, prepare, because from the ashes of burned and devastated cities, villages, houses, and from the dust of this tortured soil will rise the Polish Phoenix."

It was during these days at Cracow that those in charge of the Chopin centenary asked Paderewski to be present at Lwow for the ceremonies there. At that time, also, his symphony was to be heard for the first time in the country whose story is enclosed in its measures. For the symphony's first movement is entitled "*In Memoriam.*" Its second, a song of hope, is called "*Sursum Corda,*" and the finale is a symphonic poem based on heroic Polish melodies. At Lwow, the composer and the orator spoke with equal eloquence.

Paderewski's voice rang with determined courage as he recalled Poland's glorious history, even under long oppression. His words closed with a promise of triumph as powerful as the final pages of the symphony, as he said, "Let us brace our hearts to fresh endurance, let us adjust our minds to action, energetic, righteous; let us uplift our consciousness by faith invisible; for the nation cannot perish which has a soul so great and immortal.

"Let the oppressor hear, I do not fear him!"

Small wonder that the Russian police, when the symphony was played in Warsaw the following year, forbade the printing of any program notes referring to the significance of its themes. But by that time every Pole had heard Paderewski's words and knew the meaning of his music.

CHAPTER **6**

"THEY WILL LISTEN"

All summer long the lovely town of Morges had its share of the Swiss tourist business, but no date in the year meant more to the hotel keepers, bakers, florists and other local businessmen than July 31. It was the happiest town holiday of the year. July 31 is the feast of the great St. Ignatius Loyola, founder of the Society of Jesus. It was, therefore, Ignace Paderewski's feast day. Paderewski had a great devotion to his noble patron, and St. Ignatius' day was the occasion on which friends from all over the world gathered at Riond-Bosson to celebrate with him.

As the years passed, the Paderewski feast day parties became famous as the most brilliant gatherings in Europe, for among the guests were the world's most talented and witty people. Great care was expended on these festive occasions not only on the refreshments, which were superb, but on the entertainment, which was unique!

The celebration of July 31, 1914, was as lovingly and carefully planned as all the others, but a cloud of apprehension hung over the day. One month had passed since the assassination of the Austrian Archduke, Franz Ferdinand. This act of violence had triggered the chain of events that would lead to the catastrophe of world war. An uneasy peace was still in effect, but no one could guess how long it would last. After Mass, the day, usually devoted exclusively to fun, was punctuated by closed-door conferences with military and diplomatic leaders.

But when the time came for the evening's festivities, everyone tried to relax and forget the troubles of

the world, if only for a few hours. The dinner was
one of Antonina's and the chef's greatest triumphs.
The decorations—this year everything was ultra-
Chinese—were a delight. The dancing was especially
amusing because of the newly-imported American
ragtime. The "ragging" music was provided by eight
hands on two pianos. The hands belonged to Olga
Samaroff, Josef Hofman, Ernest Schelling, and Ru-
dolf Ganz. As for the entertainment! Schelling, who
was Paderewski's favorite pupil, was its mastermind.
At midnight he summoned the guests to the drawing
room, where chairs had been set up for the performance. Tonight, the guests were told, they were in for
an unprecedented treat—a world premiere! They
were to hear the first performance of "a symphony by
Schoenberg!" Arnold Schoenberg was the leading
composer of a type of new music that was understood
by very few people, and Paderewski was known to
turn a particularly deaf ear in its direction. Hence the
delighted laughter and applause when the audience
heard that a "Schoenberg Symphony" had mysteri-
ously turned up in manuscript at Riond-Bosson. Paderewski, for whom the entertainment was always a

Riond-Bosson

jealously guarded surprise, threw up his hands in mock horror.

To perform the new "symphony," Schelling and his fellow members of the "orchestra" had raided the kitchen and the rest of the estate for every noise-making instrument they could lay hands on: pots and pans, cups and saucers, eggbeaters and typewriters,

107

hoses and horseshoes. With Schelling's frenzied conducting to urge them on, the musicians turned in a truly superb performance. At the climax of the work, pots, pans, dishes, garden tools, everything went hurtling into a large rain barrel, with a crash that could probably be heard across Lake Geneva. Overcome by the beauty of it all, the exhausted conductor himself plunged head first into the barrel.

As the last echo of golden sound died away, as the audience gathered its collective breath to unleash a chorus of "bravo's," the telephone rang.

The telephone had been ringing all day, bringing greetings from missing friends. Why, then, was there so ominous a quality in the sound of it now? Paderewski was summoned by the butler and disappeared up the short flight of steps that led from the drawing room. A few minutes later he appeared at the top step and looked down at the guests who were now conversing in tense whispers.

"My friends," he said quietly, "the war is here."

The war had come, as inevitably it would. The cost of the next four years in human life and human misery was something so dreadful that few people could even begin to imagine it. How ironic, thought Paderewski, that in the cataclysm of war would be found the means of freeing Poland from a century and a half of bondage. "We have known it would come," he told the men who gathered in his study at dawn on August 1, "yet we are not prepared. The gigantic armies of Germany and Russia will clash on this helpless body!" He pointed a finger at the map of Poland that lay on the table before him. "But while Poland's jailers attack each other, their captive will escape!"

Yet he shuddered at the thought of what would happen to his country in the immediate future. The geographical location of Poland made it an absolute certainty that the full impact of war would fall upon the defenseless country. The armies of Poland's three masters would ravage the land and strip it bare.

Politically, too, the situation immediately became dangerous so far as Poland's future was concerned. Within two weeks after the beginning of the war, the Czar of Russia issued a proclamation offering freedom and love to his beloved Poles! "The time has come when the dream of your fathers and forefathers will

at length be realized! . . . Under the [Russian] scep-
tre Poland will come together, free in faith, in language, and in self-government! . . . With open heart,
with hand fraternally outstretched, great Russia
comes to you!"

Paderewski and his fellow-Poles could hardly keep
from laughing a very bitter laugh indeed at this sudden change of heart on the part of Russia, for Russia
had until then emphatically denied that there *was* such
a country as Poland. It couldn't be, could it, that the
Russians were hoping to line up Polish support against
Germany and Austria, by dangling the hope of freedom before the Poles? The worst of this hollow offer
was the fact that Russia was one of the allies of England and France. When the question of a free Poland
finally came up, might the allies not be unwilling to
act against one of themselves? Might they not say,
"The question of Polish freedom is settled. Russia will
take care of it!"

These problems and hundreds of others were all on
Paderewski's mind during the next hectic weeks at
Riond-Bosson, as he contemplated his country's fu-
ture—and his own. Paderewski had already made him-

self a career rich enough and rewarding enough to fill the life of any one man. Now he was standing on the brink of a second career—a greater one, he believed. "My country before everything else," he had said so many times. "After that—art!"

The group at Riond-Bosson realized that the first thing they had to do was to organize a relief committee for the Polish victims of war. They asked the great Polish writer, Henry Sienkiewicz, author of *Quo Vadis*, to manage its affairs in Switzerland. The Paderewskis themselves then prepared to leave their home and go to Paris and London. Antonina was left in charge of Riond-Bosson, which overnight had become a refugee shelter.

In Paris, Paderewski conferred with his countryman, Roman Dmowski, who was attempting to organize some sort of national committee to represent Poland before the other nations of the world.

In London he renewed old acquaintances, social and political. A peppery little Welshman named Lloyd George was Prime Minister. He thought the idea of a free, restored Poland one of the most ridiculous ideas he had ever heard. Others did not. Paderewski's friends from happier days now rallied around him to help with Polish relief work, even though England herself was beginning to feel the economic hardships of war. A Polish Relief Committee was formed and within four months had raised a quarter of a million dollars for relief. At its head was Miss Laurence Alma-Tadema, who had admired Paderewski since the long past day when she had first seen him posing for his portrait in her father's studio.

With affairs in Switzerland, Paris, and London under control, Paderewski was now free to turn his face towards the country that he firmly believed held the key to Poland's future. In January of 1915, he sailed for America.

When Paderewski returned to the United States in January of 1915 he had two missions to accomplish. The first was to raise money to feed the starving people of Poland. No one thought there was anything odd about the world-famous pianist devoting himself to the cause of his suffering countrymen. It was the sort of thing one expected of artists.

The second part of his task was much more complex. The war was only six months old. No one knew how long it would last, but some day it would be over. That much, at least, was certain. And when that day came, statesmen from all over the world would sit down in conference to draw the new boundary lines of Europe. If the dream of a free Poland were ever to become a reality, it would be then. But who among these statesmen knew or cared anything about the fate of a country that geographically had ceased to exist one hundred years ago? At the moment they had other things on their minds—such as winning a war. And in neutral America, the chief concern of responsible statesmen was the question of staying out of the war.

In Washington, D.C., Robert Lansing, the United States Secretary of State, and therefore the most important man in the field of foreign policy, was surprised one day when his secretary told him that the pianist Paderewski had asked for an appointment. He was even more surprised when the famous man arrived in his office and began to talk, eloquently he admitted, about the ideal of a united and independent Poland.

Secretary Lansing was a true diplomat. Although the question of reuniting the former country of Poland was about the last thing in the world he had time to discuss, he listened courteously. His thoughts were all negative. "This man is way out of his depth. He's a sentimental idealist. What does he know about the cold, cut-throat facts of international politics? He's trying to do something that's impossible."

As gently as he could, Lansing asked a few pointed questions. Whom did Paderewski represent? The Polish government? There was no Polish government. The Polish people? But which ones? The German-Poles? The Austrian-Poles? The Russian-Poles? There was no such thing as a unified Polish people whose ideas the statesmen of the world would respect because of sheer force of numbers. As for the Poles in America, Lansing pointed out, they were more hopelessly divided than the Poles who actually lived in the divided country! Paderewski was only too well aware of this fact. He had often smiled over the old joke that says, "Put two Poles on a sofa and you have a new political party!"

In the United States several Polish relief committees

were already in existence. Naturally each group was trying its best to snare the famous pianist for its own ranks. The minute his ship had landed, he had been besieged by their representatives. He had walked by the hour with them in Central Park, listening to each man's arguments in favor of his own point of view. He had committed himself to none of them.

The man who could actually bring off the task of unifying the American Poles would have to be a political genius, not a musical genius, Lansing thought. As he studied the flying hair and romantically flowing tie of his visitor, he decided that this was decidedly not the man to do it.

During the next few weeks Paderewski became accustomed to the faint smile with which government officials greeted him. He knew so well what they were thinking. "What does a pianist know about international affairs?"

As Paderewski prepared to cross the country and begin his tour, he felt discouraged but not despondent. The men he had seen in Washington were important men, but they were not the ones who would really count in the end. There was a man—exactly the right man—whose support he needed, the "providential man" for whom he prayed and waited. But he knew that God would send him when it was time.

The city of San Francisco was holding a great exposition. The committee had asked Paderewski to play a concert for the occasion, since he had always been San Francisco's favorite artist. When he replied that he was in the country to speak for Polish relief, not to play concerts, they willingly changed their offer. He could talk, he could play, he could do anything he liked. They in turn would guarantee him an audience of thousands who would be glad to hear whatever he had to say. It was a fine way to begin his career as a speaker, Paderewski thought. But as the day and finally the hour itself approached, he grew more and more nervous.

"What makes me think I can persuade an audience?" he asked his wife. "By playing—perhaps. But by speaking! And in English! How do I know they will even listen to me?"

Madame Paderewska's eyes did not stray an inch from the sock she was knitting. She smiled patiently and said for the tenth time that day, "They will listen."

As Paderewski walked toward the stage of the enormous auditorium that night, he longed for the blissful assurance he had once had of knowing exactly how every note was going to sound. He stepped out from the wings—and then stopped in his tracks at the breath-taking sight that greeted him.

The stage was bare except for the piano. Hanging behind the piano was an enormous flag that had been made only a day before. It covered the huge back wall of the building from one side to the other, and from ceiling to floor. A triumphant white eagle on a blood-red field! The flag of Poland!

Paderewski's nervousness vanished. He felt a great surge of confidence both for the present moment and for the future. The audience was cheering wildly, but as he walked to the front of the stage and bowed, a deep silence settled over the hall.

He said, "I have to speak to you about a country which is not yours, in a language which is not mine."

It was the first of over three hundred speeches. It was the opening of a journey that would carry him to

The flag of Poland!

every state in the country. He would travel thousands of miles to speak thousands of words. And with the unerring instinct of an artist, he had begun with a phrase that sent an electric shock through that first audience and every future audience that heard it.

"A country which is not yours—" Yet as Paderewski traveled from city to city, from platform to platform, more and more Americans began to sense a kinship with the country that did not even appear on the map. For the first time the bitter irony of the Polish situation became clear to them. Here was a country that had lost its freedom four years before America's had been declared. Yet Poland had been one of the first nations in the world to advance the beliefs on which America had been founded. "Already in the fifteenth century a self-governing country, Poland became, in 1573, a regular republic, with kings elected. In 1430, consequently 259 years before the habeas corpus of England . . . Poland established her famous law 'No man shall be detained unless legally convicted.' Our broad, liberal Constitution of 1791 preceded by 57 years the Constitution of Germany and Austria, and by 114 years the so-called Consti-

tution of Russia. And all these momentous reforms
. . . were accomplished without revolution, without
any bloodshed, without the loss of one single human
life. Does it prove our dissensions? Does it prove our
anarchy? Does it prove our inability to govern ourselves?"

"In a language which is not mine—" Yet somehow
he had made it his. Audiences that had loved Paderewski the pianist now realized that he was equally great
as an orator, although he spoke simply and without
dramatic gestures.

When he finished speaking, he would turn to the
piano and continue his plea for Poland in still another
language. He would play the music of Chopin, and
when the listeners finally left the hall, they knew that
they had lived through a unique emotional experience.

It was no wonder that money for Polish relief began to pour in. Few people who heard Paderewski
say "Give me seed for this trampled, wasted land,
bread for these starving!" could resist the appeal.
Generous America took the forgotten Polish people
to its heart. By presidential decree a special "Polish
Day" was established, because in the eyes of America

"Poland" had become synonymous with "Paderew-ski," the beloved artist who had so enriched the golden era of peace.

Although the first half of his mission had flourished beyond his greatest hopes, Paderewski felt that so far he had done very little about the second half. He had talked to plenty of government officials and diplo-mats, but they had little to offer beyond polite inter-est. Not until he had been in the United States for a year was he able to take the first sizable step. As he had known it must, it came through the intervention of one man, a man who was neither government offi-cial nor diplomat. He was the man to whom Paderew-ski would write, "It has been the dream of my life to find a providential man for my country. I am now sure that I have not been dreaming vain dreams."

CHAPTER **7**

THE PROVIDENTIAL MAN

Colonel Edward Mandell House, who had never accepted a political office, was more powerful than any man in Washington. He was the confidential adviser of President Woodrow Wilson. "His thoughts and mine are one," Wilson said of House, whom he regarded as the most unselfish, patriotic man he knew. No one in the country had a greater understanding of

European affairs than House. "A super-civilized person," the French statesman, Clemenceau, said of him, "escaped from the wilds of Texas, who sees everything, who understands everything . . . a sifting, pondering mind."

From the day he had left England, Paderewski had known that he could not succeed unless he somehow got to House and convinced him of the justice in Polish claims. But Paderewski was not the only foreigner in the country who wanted something from the Colonel. House was under constant siege by representatives of small countries who were hoping to gain something by the peace settlement. Since America was still neutral, House had to be careful in dealing with these men or even in seeing them. This is why Paderewski proceeded cautiously in his opening moves toward the Colonel. The fact that House's apartment was a three minute walk from Paderewski's hotel was an added source of frustration. So short a distance separated him from the man who could do so much for him!

Then one day early in 1916, his prayers were suddenly answered. Paderewski's discreet diplomacy had born fruit in a typical way. A Paderewski friend had wangled a letter of introduction from an Assistant Secretary of Agriculture to Mr. Robert Wooley, director of the U.S. Mint. Mr. Wooley was known to be a close friend of Colonel House. One day he sent word from Washington that he would be in New York in two days and would try to arrange a meeting between Paderewski and the Colonel. Paderewski was learning his new role in a practical way. As many a diplomat had done before and after him, he had gained his objective through a friend of a friend of a friend of the man he wanted to meet.

Mr. Wooley had sternly cautioned Paderewski against over-optimism. So his heart sank when he was greeted at the door by a radiant Madame Paderewska. "You are going to save Poland!" she cried, her beautiful eyes filled with tears. "I know it!" And as the two men walked the few blocks to House's East Fifty-third Street brownstone home, the practical man of business wondered even more at the Polish pianist's calm and complete faith in the events of the next few minutes. Well, perhaps he was right, but Wooley was inclined to doubt it.

Colonel House had marked half an hour off his tight schedule for his interview with Paderewski, so the two men did not waste time on small talk. Paderewski had been waiting a long time for this moment. He was ready for it. Pacing up and down the Colonel's library, he began to tell his story. Point by point he built his arguments for Poland, with a mixture of logic and eloquence that an experienced lawyer might have envied.

The half hour flew by. Nervously Mr. Wooley looked at his watch and then glanced at the Colonel. "Let him go on," House muttered. "Don't interrupt him."

An hour passed and then another hour. Whatever Colonel House's later appointments were, they were cancelled. Never in his career of listening to people who wanted something had he heard a man plead his cause so irresistibly.

When he had made his last point, Paderewski stopped and waited for the Colonel to speak. House's part in the two hour conversation was limited to three sentences, but they were the most beautiful words Paderewski had ever heard. "You have convinced me," he said, rising and holding out his hand. "I promise you to help Poland if I can. And I believe I can."

It was the beginning of a profound friendship between the two men, one so eloquent, and one so silent. And with the Colonel completely won over to his side, the door to the White House stood open to Paderewski at last. By the summer of 1916 House felt that the time had come to introduce the pianist to President Wilson. He arranged to have the Paderewskis invited to a diplomatic dinner at the White House.

Woodrow Wilson was a scholar and a statesman. He had been a college president before he went into politics. Such a man, Paderewski believed, would understand the justice of his cause.

There was great excitement after dinner that night when guests saw the piano in the East Room being opened. Was Paderewski really going to play? He was, they were told, since the President had asked him to do so.

Although President Wilson did not know a great deal about music, it did not take any special knowledge to get the message that the Polish artist was try-

Woodrow Wilson had won an ally.

ing to convey by means of Chopin's music. Paderewski and Chopin had become partners in this enterprise, and never had the two worked together so eloquently. As Wilson and Paderewski talked briefly together after the performance, the pianist felt that he had won his country another powerful ally.

It worked both ways. Wilson, too, had won an ally. 1916 was an election year. Paderewski campaigned actively for Wilson's reelection all during the fall. Many Polish voters, following the lead of the Polish clergy, were Republicans. Paderewski convinced them that their country's first real hope in a hundred years depended on a victory for Wilson. In the end he delivered the large Polish vote almost one hundred percent.

On the day before elections, when the campaigner had expected to relax a little, came shattering news from Europe. Germany had issued a proclamation declaring that Poland was a free and independent nation. The freedom and independence, of course, were the affectionate gift of the German government. The story behind the "gift" was actually a simple one. Germany had previously shown no sign of any such good will to the Polish people. Far from it. As soon as the Russians had been driven out, the German and Austrian leaders had gathered over a map of Poland and had once more divided it up, this time in a two-way split—one half for Germany, one half for Austria. Now suddenly they were declaring the country re-united and free! Why?

Paderewski knew why. It was not Polish freedom the German leaders wanted. It was Polish manpower. They were convinced that if they presented Poland

with independence, a million Polish volunteers would
gratefully flock to enlist in the German army and
could be used to fight the Russians in the East. The
other reason for the move was a more subtle danger.
If the Poles appeared to accept the offer and consented
to be taken under the loving wing of Germany, then
America and the Allies would lose interest in the cause
of Polish freedom. Poland herself would be regarded
as a friend of the enemy.

Paderewski saw through the trick easily. "This
means only more suffering for my people," he told
House. "It means that another army will be raised and
that there will be more killing and more devastation!"
He realized that everything he had won during the
past few years was in danger of being destroyed in
one day. Unless he acted quickly. But what could he
do? Never before had he felt so cruelly his lack of
real authority. If only he were the official spokesman
for some truly representative Polish groups, so that
when he spoke a firm majority of Poles spoke with
him.

There was only one thing to be said for the fact
that he had everything to lose: he could afford to take

a desperate gamble. Cable lines buzzed between New York and Paris, Paris and Chicago, Chicago and New York. Within a few hours a statement was issued and flashed to every Allied country. The German offer was rejected, flatly and permanently. The message was signed by Paderewski and was approved by the Paris Committee and by several groups in the United States.

But what about the rest of his countrymen, Paderewski wondered. What about the millions of poor Poles who were not trained thinkers, who might not see the worm in the shining German apple? Would they support him, or would they demand the right to seize their freedom no matter who offered it to them?

He soon had his answer. Every Polish society in the country immediately voted to make Paderewski its official representative. They gave him full power of attorney to make decisions and to act for them in all political matters. From then on, when he spoke he was speaking with the voice of three million Polish-Americans.

Of everything that Paderewski had done, this was the coup that really made its mark on official Washington. "The first direct evidence of his capacity as a leader which impressed me," wrote an observer, "was his successful efforts to unite the jealous and bickering Polish factions in the United States . . . I am convinced that Mr. Paderewski was the only Pole who could have overcome this menace . . . His entire freedom from personal ambition made him the one man about whom the Poles, regardless of factions, appeared to be willing to rally. It was a great achievement, a triumph of personality."

The man who wrote this was Robert Lansing, the Secretary of State who had once smiled when an eccentric piano player had tried to talk to him about Poland.

The exhausting events of November 5 and 6 should have provided quite enough excitement and tension for any two days in a man's life. But they were only one part of the affairs that occupied him during those forty-eight hours. November 6, remember, was election day!

Woodrow Wilson had gone to Shadow Lawn, his summer house on the New Jersey shore, to wait for the election returns in comparative peace. It was a trying day for him, following a hard, bitter campaign. It was a day on which he chose his visitors with care. One of them was Paderewski.

In the quiet study at Shadow Lawn the two men talked for nearly an hour. Wilson spoke of his idealist's dreams of world peace and mutual trust between nations. He listened attentively while Paderewski, in turn, described his hopes for his own country. The President asked searching, practical questions. How could Poland survive without an outlet to the sea? Paderewski and House had often discussed this point over a map of Europe. He explained their ideas to the President. When the interview was over, Wilson said solemnly, "My dear Paderewski, I can tell you that Poland will be resurrected and will exist again!"

Paderewski went home exhausted but intensely happy. It had been quite a pair of days! He longed to go to bed, but the election returns were coming in faster and faster now and he could not settle down for the night until he knew for certain that everything was going as expected. He heard the then familiar—and now extinct—cry for which all America had once waited. "Extra! Extra! Read all about it!" But the rest of the newsboy's cry was a catastrophe. "Wilson defeated! Hughes elected!"

Wilson defeated? Wilson who had just promised him his country's freedom? For two years he had worked inch by inch in the direction of the words he had heard only a few hours before. And now it meant nothing.

It was a cruel night, unnecessarily cruel as it turned out. By five the next morning the newspapers were out with a somewhat different story. Wilson had not been defeated. The Extra-hungry papers had simply neglected to wait for the California votes to be counted!

"I can tell you that Poland will be resurrected and will exist again," Wilson had said. And the promise was still good.

CHAPTER **8**

THE THIRTEENTH POINT

Paderewski was playing a war relief benefit the next afternoon. He had played so little except his Chopin since his return to the United States that he was preparing for the much-heralded Carnegie Hall recital with even greater care than usual. It was Monday, January 8, 1917.

While he was practicing, a message came from down the street that Colonel House would like to see him. Very little else would have taken him away from the piano at that moment, but he was soon in the Colonel's study.

Colonel House came quickly to the point, as usual. "Next Thursday I am going to leave for Washington, and I wish to have with me your memorandum on Poland."

What the Colonel meant was this: he had decided that the time had come to present President Wilson with a full-scale study of the Polish situation. What he needed from Paderewski was a memorandum telling exactly what he wanted for his country and how he thought it should be accomplished. It was the sort of document that half a dozen trained diplomats might work over for three weeks!

Paderewski felt as though a large mallet had just thumped him on the head. "Thursday! But I have my recital tomorrow! And besides, it is impossible to prepare such a document without the necessary data, and besides—"

"I must have that memorandum by Thursday morning!"

Paderewski had by this time learned one thing about the Colonel. He might be a man of few words, but he meant every one of them.

He walked back to his hotel slowly. At all costs, he told himself, he must keep his wits about him and not panic. During World War II there was a Seabee slogan that would have appealed to Paderewski, had he heard it. "The difficult we do immediately. The impossible takes a little longer." He himself operated along these lines. This job was impossible. It would take a while. He went up to his rooms and began practicing for four hours.

The program of that Tuesday afternoon recital included the Beethoven C minor piano sonata, Op. 111. This is one of the most taxing of all the sonatas in the kind of intellectual demands it makes on the performer. In addition to the Beethoven he played the Schumann "Butterflies," one of his favorite recital pieces, and his own piano sonata Op. 21. Shorter works by Chopin, Liszt, Mendelssohn and his composer-friend Stojowski completed the program. And as usual in a Paderewski recital, the encores he played so generously were almost as extensive as the printed program.

Next morning the critics were enthusiastic about

the pianist's "bravura performance." They spoke of the wild delight of the audience which agreed to go home only after the lights in the hall had been turned off. It was, in other words, "a typical Paderewski recital audience," wrote the man from the *Tribune*. In it were "men and women of society, musicians, and many young persons, even boys and girls who will grow up to tell their juniors about the time 'when I heard Paderewski.' "

Yet neither the critic nor the boys and girls knew what a fantastic scene they had just witnessed: Paderewski locked in absolute concentration on Beethoven and Schumann and the others, while the fate of his country waited silently for him on his desk.

When the recital was finally over—and he did not deprive the audience of so much as one bow—he went home and ate dinner. Then he went to work on the memorandum. Thirty-six hours later—at eight A.M. on Thursday morning—it was delivered to Colonel House. Paderewski went to bed for the first time since Monday night.

His fatigue seemed well worth it a week later when the Colonel came back from Washington. "The President was very much pleased with your memorandum," he said. "Now get ready. The first shot will be fired very soon!"

On January 22 President Wilson addressed Congress on "Essential Terms of Peace in Europe." Paderewski, who was touring in the South at the time, picked up a newspaper the next day and read these words: "No peace can last or ought to last which does not recognize and accept the principle that governments derive all their just powers from the consent of the governed, and that no right anywhere exists to hand people about from sovereignty to sovereignty as if they were property. I take it for granted . . . that statesmen everywhere are agreed that there should be a united, independent, and autonomous Poland, and that henceforth inviolable security of life and worship . . . should be guaranteed to all people who have lived hitherto under the power of governments devoted to a faith and purpose hostile to their own."

The words swam before his eyes. For the first time, the fate of Poland had been publicly mentioned as an official concern of the United States government.

On April 2, 1917, President Wilson came to an

anguished but inevitable decision. He called upon the Congress to declare war against Germany. Full mobilization of the country's manpower was immediately begun. Two days later, Paderewski, addressing the "Union of Polish Falcons," the most important Polish-American group, called for the formation of a separate Polish army, to fight side by side with the Allies. An independent Polish army, he felt, would prove to the world as nothing else could that there was truly a Polish nation waiting for its moment of rebirth. After almost insurmountable difficulties, he finally won his point, and the governments of France and the United States allowed him to go ahead with his plans for the formation of the army. Two training camps for Polish volunteers were founded, and soon twenty-two thousand Polish-Americans had enlisted in "the Army of Kosciuszko." For help in transporting so large a number of men to Europe, Paderewski turned to the Secretary of the Navy, Josephus Daniels. He, in turn, knew just the man to assign to the Paderewski case—a young Assistant Secretary named Franklin Delano Roosevelt whose admiration for the pianist dated from childhood. With Roosevelt's enthusiastic, red-tape-cutting aid, Paderewski's volunteers were quickly sent to Europe. There they joined with the European Poles to form an army numbering nearly one hundred thousand men, fighting under the banner of the white eagle.

Statesmen who had once believed that Poles could never be united were now confronted by the fact of a hundred thousand men joined by a common oath. "I swear before Almighty God, One in Three, to be faithful to my country Poland, one and indivisible, and to be ready to give my life for the holy cause of its unification and liberation. I swear to defend my flag to the last drop of my blood, to observe military discipline, to obey my leaders, and by my conduct to maintain the honor of a Polish soldier."

The Polish army paid tribute to Paderewski in a superb and moving way. His name was inscribed on the membership list of each company. Every day at roll call, when the name "Ignace Jan Paderewski" was read, one hundred thousand voices shouted back, "Present!" This honor had been paid to a soldier only once before in history—to Napoleon. It had never before been paid to a civilian.

And then at last came the day on which the unselfish labors of the last three years bore glorious fruit. On January 8, 1918, as the war entered its last phase, President Wilson spoke to Congress on the peace that lay ahead. He offered a fourteen point program for what he hoped could be a just and permanent settlement of the world's disputes. The thirteenth of these points was this: "An independent Polish state should be erected which should include the territories inhabited by indisputably Polish populations, which should be assured a free and secure access to the sea, and whose political and economic independence and territorial integrity should be guaranteed by international covenant."

As Paderewski read the electric words, he realized that they were taken almost verbatim from the memorandum he had written for Colonel House after his Carnegie Hall recital exactly one year before. Paderewski's work in America had been crowned with a success that not even he, full of faith as he was, could have imagined.

In Poland, news of the thirteenth point brought life-saving hope to the hearts of the beleaguered Polish people. On an entirely different level an earlier incident had already kindled a new flame of courage in the hearts of the people of Warsaw. It had happened during the final rout of Russian troops by an advancing German army. To gain time for their retreat, the Russians blew up the Poniatowski Bridge that spanned the river Vistula in the very heart of the city. The devastating roar of dynamite smashed windows and shook buildings for miles around. Even the solid Zamek shuddered to its foundation stones. The blast almost uprooted the statues in Palace Square. As the powerful vibrations ripped past him, King Sigismund tottered but stood firm. Yet even in their fright the people who ran through the square seeking shelter could not fail to understand his message. Soon the magical words were flying through the city. *"Sigismund has shaken his sword!"*

At last the signing of the Armistice on November 11, 1918, brought the long horror to an end: Paderewski's work in the United States was over, the greatest tour in his career a complete success. The next step in his mission would have to be carried out in Paris, where the statesmen of the world would soon

The warship sped toward Danzig.

gather to write treaties and to rearrange the border-
lines of Europe.

In Arthur Balfour, the British Foreign Secretary,
Paderewski had a powerful friend. The experienced
statesman now gave him some strong advice. It was
essential, as Paderewski knew better than anyone else,
that Poland be represented at the Conference table.
But the Allies would never recognize a Polish government unless they felt that it truly represented all factions in Poland. At the moment most Allied leaders
leaned toward Dmowski's Polish Committee in Paris.
But others were asking, "What about Pilsudski?"

What, indeed, about Pilsudski! A hundred times a
day the name drifted across Paderewski's mind like
an ominous shadow.

Józef Pilsudski, the soldier-hero of Poland, had
fought his country's enemies for years on home
ground. He had escaped from both Russian and German prison camps to organize a Polish army and a
Polish underground. At the end of the war he had
marched triumphantly into Warsaw and been ac-
claimed Chief of State. The government he had organized was strongly socialist, almost communist in

character. It represented the left-wing factions in Poland, just as Dmowski's Polish National Committee represented the right-wing factions. Naturally the peace negotiators would not do business with both groups.

"Someone," Balfour said, "must unite these factions. Someone must go into Poland and persuade Pilsudski to cooperate with Dmowski to form a government that is truly representative of all Poles." Obviously there was only one man in the world who had any hope at all of accomplishing such an assignment.

On Christmas Day the British warship that had carried the Paderewskis safely through the treacherous mine-infested waters of the North Sea dropped anchor in Danzig, Poland's ancient seaport.

Danzig was in German territory and the Germans were not in the least enthusiastic about welcoming the man who was trying as hard as he could to relieve them of their share of Polish land. In the city of Poznań to which Paderewski proceeded from Danzig, a procession of school children carrying Polish flags was fired on by sniping Prussian soldiers. The windows of Paderewski's hotel room were shattered by flying bullets, while he himself calmly tied his necktie. Street-fighting between Poles and Prussians immediately broke out and lasted for three days. "There is no doubt," Paderewski wrote to Colonel House, "that the whole affair was organized by the Germans in order to create new difficulties for the Peace Conference."

But no amount of threats and terrorism could stop the people of Poland from lining the railroad tracks between Poznań and Warsaw to cheer and shout and weep tears of joy while they waited in the snow to catch a glimpse of the man whose name had shone like a beacon of hope for four devastating years.

Paderewski reached Warsaw on New Year's Eve. The ovation that he received from the jubilant city was heart-warming, but it was not really significant. Tens of thousands of people in Warsaw might be parading the streets in his honor; but the success or failure of his mission depended on one man alone. On the first day of the hopeful New Year, Paderewski presented himself at the Belvedere Palace for his first meeting with Marshal Józef Pilsudski.

CHAPTER **9**

REBIRTH OF A NATION

If a modern "electronic brain" were fed data about
every statesman of the twentieth century and then
asked to pick out the two men most completely opposite and uncongenial, it would without a moment's
hesitation settle on Józef Pilsudski and Ignace Jan
Paderewski. Even before their meeting each man had
a fairly good idea of what the other man was like.

147

Now for the first time they could size each other up in person.

Pilsudski, eying Paderewski's elegant clothes and quietly assured manner, recalled that this man was the darling of a capitalistic society in whose image he would try to rebuild Poland. Paderewski, noting the Marshal's rough, purposely shabby uniform, drooping mustaches, and abrupt, nervous behavior, remembered that this bold revolutionary had spent most of his adult life in prison, or in hiding, or in working under cover, always in the shadows of conspiracy. He was the sort of man who would stop at nothing, including murder, to gain his objective because he firmly believed that if the end was good, then the means were unimportant. Yet there was one point of agreement between them, Paderewski reflected, and surely it was a strong enough basis for cooperation. Each man, in his own way, loved his country and would gladly have given his life for her.

By the end of the exhausting interview Paderewski had come to the conclusion that this was not enough. Pilsudski remained absolutely unshaken in his refusal to have anything to do with Dmowski's Committee.

Poland, he believed, belonged to the proletariat—the working man—alone. He would not admit that any other class of people had any right to be represented in the new government. As to the question of Allied recognition, he simply brushed it aside. He could take care of Poland all by himself, he seemed to imply.

It was a frustrating two hours.

The next day Paderewski left for Cracow, convinced that his mission had failed. But at three o'clock on the morning after his arrival, he was roused from sleep by a special messenger from Pilsudski. The Marshal, he was informed, requested his immediate return to Warsaw for further negotiations.

What could have happened, Paderewski thought, to change Pilsudski's mind even to this small extent?

What had happened was this: on January 4, representatives of the American Relief Administration had arrived in Warsaw to study conditions and to discuss terms with Pilsudski. The starving people of Europe had good reason to be familiar with the heroic work of the A.R.A. which had already saved millions of lives during that cruel winter of armistice.

In charge of the mission to Warsaw was Vernon Kellogg, gifted both as a scientist and an administrator. Somehow he managed to get the point across to the iron-willed Marshal that if he expected American Relief supplies and money to feed and clothe the desperate Polish people, he would have to find a way of cooperating with Paderewski and the Paris Committee. Faced with so practical a necessity, Pilsudski capitulated and asked Paderewski to help him form a representative government. Paderewski himself was named Prime Minister and Minister of Foreign Affairs. Pilsudski remained "Chief of State." It was a rather all-inclusive title.

The Americans were as good as their word. Better, in fact, because once they had reported back to their chief in Paris about the ghastly conditions in Poland, miles and miles of red tape were instantly cut in order to rush in the first supplies. Within a few weeks a life-giving stream of food, clothing, fuel, and medical supplies were pouring steadily into the country. Even Pilsudski was impressed. The A.R.A did its best for all suffering countries. But there seemed to be something special—almost personal—about its feeling for Poland, even though there was not yet an officially recognized Polish government. The pianist was a nuisance, Pilsudski must have thought privately, but he had his uses if his popularity made the Americans so generous.

What Pilsudski did not know was that there was indeed a personal attitude involved in the work of the American Relief Administration for Poland. For at the head of the organization was a man with a long memory—a former Stanford University engineering student who had once taken a flyer in the business of staging concerts.

Paderewski had completely forgotten that he had once saved a young man named Herbert Hoover from great financial distress. But Herbert Hoover had never forgotten it. The $400 debt that had meant so much to the student and so little to the artist had now been paid a thousandfold.

As Prime Minister of Poland, Paderewski moved his household into the Zamek. Did he remember the many times that the young music student had passed the royal palace and prayed for the day when a Polish leader would once more be in residence there? Perhaps. But Paderewski was too busy to spend much time reminiscing. The work of forming first a National Council of a hundred men and then a coalition cabinet of sixteen was incredibly difficult. In the course of his former career he had grown accustomed to long, hard work, but it was nothing compared to this! Poles, as we have seen, were not the easiest people in the world with whom to do business politically. And complicating life almost beyond endurance was Pilsudski. The Chief enjoyed long, drawn-out, usually pointless conferences that accomplished nothing except the complete exhaustion of the Prime Minister. He enjoyed them most at two or three o'clock in the morning, preferably just after Paderewski had finally managed to retire for the night.

"There is a smell of sulphur in the air whenever that man walks into a room!" Paderewski said, and he looked forward with increasing eagerness to the day when he could leave Warsaw for Paris and the Conference. What a joy not to be in the same city as Józef Pilsudski!

If the full story of Paderewski's accomplishments

at the Paris Peace Conference were told in this book, there would scarcely be room in it for anything else. The work of the next three months was the climax and the crowning achievement of his second career.

When Paderewski finally reached Paris, the Conference was in its eleventh week. His unavoidable delay in Poland, he quickly realized, had been a costly one. Dmowski had done his best in presenting the Polish claims. His five hour speech to the delegates was acknowledged as a masterful and scholarly treatise. But here was Dmowski himself to tell Paderewski that the Polish questions were all but decided and decided in the negative! Somehow nothing was going according to plan. Hostility, open and hidden, dogged his best efforts. "There is nothing to be done about it," he announced flatly. "Everything is settled." The opposition of Lloyd George to every one of his points, for example, practically guaranteed failure. What nation would go against the British leader just because of a minor issue like Poland?

Poor Paderewski, weary from months of trying to establish order in Pilsudski's peculiar brand of chaos, now realized that he had a tremendous job of politi-

Nothing was going according to plan.

cal "fence-mending" to do in Paris. For the problem was Dmowski himself. The small nations at the Conference—those whose main business was asking rather than dispensing favors—had to depend to an enormous degree on influence. And influence was largely a question of personality. In personality Dmowski was sheer disaster. Not only did his cold and academic manner do little to win him friends among the delegates, but his terrible anti-Semitism won him active enemies among Jewish and non-Jewish delegates alike. And of all the delegates who hated Dmowski, Lloyd George hated him the most. So irked, in fact, was the fierce little Welshman that Paderewski's arrival only succeeded in rousing him to greater heights of anti-Polish feeling. "After all," he said, "what can you expect from a country that sends as its representative a pianist!"

Paderewski decided to start repairing the damage at the very top. Immediately after his arrival he paid a call on the powerful President of the Conference, Georges Clemenceau—the "tiger of France."

The present "tiger" met the former "lion" with a ghost of a twinkle in his stern eyes. "Are you, by chance," he asked solemnly, "a cousin of the famous pianist Paderewski?"

Paderewski, with equal solemnity, bowed and said, "I am the very man, Mr. President."

Clemenceau sighed deeply. "And you, the famous artist, have become merely a Prime Minister! What a comedown!"

The two men laughed as they shook hands warmly. They were off to a good start.

It was not long before nearly every delegate to the Conference—even Lloyd George—came to the conclusion that the Polish question must definitely be reconsidered before any final decision was made. Paderewski quickly became one of the most admired and therefore influential men in Paris. He was useful, too, as it developed. President Wilson and Colonel House sought his help in explaining some American attitudes to the Europeans, while the European delegates could always count on him to interpret their feelings for the Americans. More than any other man in Paris, Paderewski belonged both to the old world and the new.

"He came to Paris," Colonel House later wrote, "in the minds of many as an incongruous figure, whose place was on the concert stage, and not as one to be reckoned with in the settlement of a torn and distracted world. He left Paris, in the minds of his colleagues, a statesman, an incomparable orator, a linguist, and one who had the history of Europe better in hand than any of his brilliant associates."

One of the delegates, a smooth, professional orator, summed it all up rather nicely after a particularly wonderful speech by Paderewski. "Ah," he sighed to a group of his colleagues, "if we could play as Paderewski speaks!"

The gains that Paderewski eventually won for his country were not all that he had hoped for, but they were far greater gains than any other man in the world could have made. They represented, as one statesman put it, "a triumph of personality." Matters of boundaries, perhaps, left something to be desired, but these were not the major issue. The establishment of Poland as a nation, free and independent among the nations of the world—this was the major issue, and this was finally brought about on June 28, 1919, when the Treaty of Versailles was at last presented to the delegates for their signatures.

"What M. Paderewski has done for Poland will

The Treaty of Versailles was signed.

cause eternal gratitude," wrote Secretary of State, Robert Lansing. ". . . His career is one that deserves to be remembered . . . by every man to whom love of country and loyalty to a great cause stand forth as the noblest attributes of human character."

In the Hall of Mirrors at Versailles, a roar of applause and approval greeted Paderewski as he stepped forward to sign the treaty for Poland. No other delegate except those of the "big four" nations received such an ovation. But Paderewski's ears were accustomed to the sound of applause, and it was probably the last thing in his mind as he signed. His whole life had been directed toward this moment. He had worked, he had prayed unceasingly for the new life of his country. Now it was an accomplished fact, acknowledged by the whole world, witnessed by a stroke of his own pen.

Paderewski's career as a statesman was drawing to an end. It lasted only six months longer, and the half year was a bitter anti-climax. When the Paderewskis returned to Warsaw they found the atmosphere unbearably hostile. Now that Pilsudski had "used" his rival to gain Allied support, he was determined to get him out of the way as quickly as possible.

Growing opposition of the meanest kind blocked Paderewski's attempts to build an honorable, democratic government for his country. Pilsudski had little interest in democracy and no interest at all in maintaining the peace. He yearned for the smell of powder again, and he planned to strike for further Polish gains by making war on Russia. But first he must eliminate the peace-loving Prime Minister.

Political intrigue is a merciless game. Paderewski found himself attacked through the two things he loved most in the world: his faith and his wife. Anti-clerical feeling ran high among the socialists of the country. They used Paderewski's staunch and well-known devotion to the Church to "prove" that he was a "tool" of the clergy and was therefore, somehow, dedicated to the enslavement of the working man. It was a fantastic charge from start to finish, but people believe what they want to believe, and disgruntled elements in the Sejm—the Polish assembly—eagerly spread the story.

Even more cruel were the charges leveled against

Mme. Paderewska, she who had worked herself almost to the breaking point not only to ease her husband's arduous life, but to further the cause of Polish relief. She was accused of undue interference in matters of state, of being a bad influence on the Prime Minister, of any vindictive thing that could be thought of to discredit her husband.

A man of Paderewski's moral courage can weather almost any attack made against him, but the abuse of his wife cut him to the heart. For weeks he wrestled with his conscience. He was thinking, as usual, first of Poland; last, of himself. If he stepped aside now, would it not end the terrible dissensions that rocked the newborn country? But if he did so, would he not be deserting his country when she needed him, deserting her, perhaps, out of a selfish, if natural, longing for personal peace?

At last, on December 5, 1919, Paderewski announced his resignation from office. A few days earlier, at a wildly agitated meeting of the Sejm, his government had received a vote of confidence, but the vote had been carried by a very slim majority. Too slim a majority, Paderewski felt, to represent a true mandate of the people, particularly since one of the parties that voted against him in the Sejm actually had more followers, numerically, than any of the parties who voted in his favor. If he stayed on, nothing could follow but further discord. If he left now, then surely the country would somehow make her way to internal peace and unity.

Paderewski generously agreed to the panic-stricken request of the Sejm that he try to form a new cabinet. Then he quietly left Warsaw, and after five years of voluntary exile returned to his beloved home on the shining Swiss lake.

CHAPTER **10**

"AFTER THAT—ART!"

An announcement the world had been hoping to hear came from Paderewski on July 14—Bastille Day —1922. As he boarded the *S.S. Savoie* in New York for a trip back to Europe, he announced that in the fall of that year he would return to the United States to resume his concert career. He had not played in public for five years, not since the night he played in the Metropolitan Opera House at a special concert in honor of the French hero, Marshal Joffre. But now he was ready to move back to Carnegie Hall and the other concert platforms of the world. Or at least he would be ready, he felt, after four more months of the kind of hard work he had been doing behind closed doors for over two years.

Although certain of his friends advised against the step, the fact of the matter was that Paderewski had no choice. He had to return to the stage because it was the only way he knew how to make a living. He had to work for a living because he had no money. He, who had been the richest artist appearing before the public, was now all but penniless. Nearly all of his great fortune had been given away to the war-hungry people of Europe.

The announcement created a sensation. Paderewski was returning to the stage! Newspaper editorials around the world—and even his close friends and staunchest admirers—asked the same question: would his second concert career be a triumph or a failure? Yet the answer should have been clear to anyone who gave a moment's thought to Paderewski's life and work. Clearly he would never have made the decision to return to the scenes of his former greatness if he had not been sure of his own powers and of his ability to use them again as fully as before.

But never before had Paderewski spent more painstaking hours on his beloved music than he did in the months just before his second Carnegie Hall debut. The great French violinist, Jacques Thibaud, who crossed the Atlantic with him, said that Paderewski even sacrificed his favorite pastime of bridge in favor of extra hours of practicing.

It was thirty-one years, almost to the very day, since his well-remembered debut in Carnegie Hall in 1891. Now, on November 22, 1922, he walked out on the famous stage to begin again. This time an audience that months before had bought every seat in the house filled the hall with a great cheering at his entrance, and kept up the applause until he seated himself at the Steinway and struck the few chords with which he always liked to quiet his listeners. That he was nervous was certain. But that his fingers had every ounce of the control, of the magic singing sound, and the thundering excitement they had had in the past was clear to him and to his audience. It was clear, also, to the critics, who were unanimous as they sought, almost desperately, to describe the mature playing of this man who was now so much more than a pianist.

There was no dissent anywhere from the critical opinions. But there was one special friend who, under unique circumstances, summed it up better than any other. He was Georges Clemenceau, France's wartime premier.

On the night before his own return concert in Carnegie Hall, Paderewski had gone to the Metropolitan Opera House to hear Clemenceau speak. But Clemenceau had to make another speech on November 22 and had not been able to hear the great triumph of Paderewski's return. When Paderewski's concert was over, he was driven to the home of Charles Dana Gibson, a fashionable artist of the day, with whom Clemenceau was staying. There, the two men greeted each other with the deepest affection.

Paderewski said to Clemenceau, "You are the greatest man I ever knew. You told them the truth in a splendid way of which you alone are capable."

He was referring to Clemenceau's speech at the Metropolitan Opera, when the "tiger of France" had called upon America to help Europe in the difficult postwar days.

"No, no, you are the greatest man," Clemenceau replied. "At the peace conference you made such a wonderful speech that I was nearly moved to tears." Then the old Frenchman paused. "I missed your concert," he said apologetically. "When will you play for me?"

"Master," Paderewski answered. "I will do anything for you. I will play for you now!" And for nearly an hour, the man who had only a short time before played for three hours in Carnegie Hall played in the half-light of the Gibson mansion. When it was over, Clemenceau said, "Marvelous, marvelous. You are not only a great musician and a great statesman, but a great poet also."

From New York, Paderewski's tour led him across America, as it had so many times in the past. His private car again became a familiar sight on the railroad tracks of the country. Again switchmen, brakemen, and the freight handlers across the country were treated to the glorious sounds that came from this very special Pullman car. In Minneapolis, Paderewski played an entire impromptu recital in the car one day for ten nuns who could not attend his regular concert. Sitting at his upright, with the noises of switching cars and passing engines for background, Paderewski played as if he were on the stage of a great auditorium. And surely he had never had a more appreciative audience.

The world's capitals, political and musical, saw and heard Paderewski once more as he traveled from Hawaii to London in the old, familiar crossing and recrossing pattern. Honors came to him, more than were ever given to any pianist before or since. Universities vied with each other to give him honorary degrees. One, from New York University, had to be delivered to him in his hotel room when he was too ill to leave it for the formal convocation. To the University's Chancellor, Paderewski said, with a smile, "You have come to a sick man to make a doctor of him!"

Paderewski easily recovered from a sudden appendectomy, in the fall of 1929, and made one of the

Ignace Paderewski, 70 years of age

longest of all his American tours the following year, playing 87 concerts in the winter of 1930–31. The death of his wife in January, 1934, was less upsetting to Paderewski than some of his friends had feared it might be, because for five years before she died, Mme. Paderewska had suffered from a loss of memory and her tragic illness had actually withdrawn her from all the activities in which for over 35 years she had played so busy a role.

On his tours, Paderewski played many benefits for war veterans. In the years when the depression spread across the U.S. and Europe, he was always glad to play concerts whose proceeds went to unemployed musicians. One of these, in Madison Square Garden in 1932, raised nearly $50,000. And in the midst of his renewed career, Paderewski kept in intimate touch with the political development in Poland and throughout Europe.

One of the greatest of his speeches was given in May, 1932, at a banquet in his honor in New York City. Broadcast across the entire country, Paderewski's address that day was a magnificently outlined, superbly delivered history and analysis of the so-called Polish Corridor. His country's vital need for an outlet to the Baltic Sea was at stake, and Poland's position and rights were being threatened. The entire speech was later published in *Foreign Affairs*. It was built as a master symphony is built, with its principal themes stated in varying manner during its course, and its closing pages rising to a superb climax. As he reached its final lines, Paderewski said:

"We do not wish to be crippled or enslaved again. We will never accept so monstrous an injury, no matter by whom inflicted. The territory restored to us is justly ours. And we will stand by it with all our strength and uphold it by all our means. For if that restoration is wrong, then the partitions of Poland were right—and nobody should expect us to subscribe to such an inquitous verdict . . .

"We do not want war. Everyone in Poland is longing for peace. We need peace more than any other country in the whole world. Nevertheless, if a war—and I am speaking now not as an official person, because I am not an official; I am a plain citizen, and I assume my own responsibility—if a war, I repeat it, by a formal declaration or by surprise is imposed on us, we shall defend ourselves." Once again Paderewski was speaking the language of prophecy, though seven years still lay ahead before Poland would once again be invaded, this time by the armies of Hitler.

The year 1936 brought a brand new career into a life already crowned in two widely separated areas, music and politics. On August 8, Paderewski, the movie star, was born. For months, Paderewski's chief aide had been working quietly, without Paderewski's knowledge, to arrange the making of a movie about Paderewski. Finally when negotiations with a British company had reached a stage where Paderewski's consent was necessary, the subject was brought up and met with none of the resistance that had been expected. Despite his lifelong dislike of bright lights, especially while playing, Paderewski spent two weeks on a movie lot outside of London making what is really a weakly sentimental production entitled "Moonlight Sonata." Its one distinguishing feature is the ennobling sight and sound of the great artist moving through a few scenes.

The movie did have the effect of returning Paderewski to at least semi-public playing for the first time since the death of Mme. Paderewska, two years before. Late in 1938, Paderewski agreed to a short tour of England, where he played with ease and vigor. Their surprise turned to genuine dismay, however, a few weeks later when Paderewski announced his return to the U.S. for the early spring of 1939. The cold, undeniable fact was that Paderewski once again needed money. He could only earn enough to meet his obligations by returning to the United States at the age of 79 to play again for the thousands who clamored to hear him. He had never saved any money for the days when he might need it for himself. There had always seemed some better reason for giving it away. Against this real need was Paderewski's rapidly failing health. In her diary, a friend said of him at this time, "He looks so feeble and moves about with such difficulty that I simply don't see how he can contemplate a concert tour of the U.S., of all places. . . . How on earth will the President walk on the stage during his recitals? Surely not with the support of his cane, which he uses to get from room to room!"

Studio 8-H of Radio City

He did come to the United States and played the first concert of his 20th tour in that country in Studio 8-H of Radio City, before an invited audience of several hundred and a radio audience that was estimated at fifty million. Olin Downes said of Paderewski's playing of the *Moonlight Sonata* on that day, "We had not heard him play this music with such tonal beauty and poetical effect." The program included Liszt and Chopin, and at the end, naturally, *the* Minuet, of which the audience literally forced an encore.

Several more concerts followed, each of them packed to the rafters. Then came May 25, the day of the final concert scheduled for Madison Square Garden. It had been sold out for days, and as the hands of the clock moved down to 8:30, more than 15,000 people full of a special expectancy waited for the famous old man to appear. 8:35 came, and 8:40, and still they waited. A little before 9 o'clock, an announcement came over the Garden's loudspeakers. "Ladies and gentlemen, Mr. Paderewski has had a slight heart attack in his dressing room, and his doctor is moving him back to his private car." Slowly, not quite believing what had happened, the crowd quietly began to leave, many of them without any thought of getting their money back, for already someone had suggested that a fund in honor of Paderewski could be started with the money that was in the box office. Paderewski had played his last concert.

But still there was strength in the grand old lion. And he would need every ounce of it. Five days after his collapse, Paderewski was strong enough to sail for France on the *Normandie*. After resting in Paris for several weeks, he returned to his beloved Riond-Bosson. On August 1, 1914, he had once stood and said, "My friends, the war is here." And here, on September 1, 1939, twenty-five years and one month later, the news came to him that the Nazi army, at Hitler's orders, had invaded Poland. On that day Paderewski broke his long-standing rule never to listen to the radio. The only set in the villa was brought down to the dining room where, throughout the day, it poured out its tragic reports: Warsaw and many other Polish cities being laid waste by German bombs. His prophecy of a quarter of a century before had come true all too soon!

Now the blows came faster, with the fall of France, and, in Paderewski's opinion, with the complete failure of the machinery of the League of Nations to function as his old friend, Woodrow Wilson, had intended it to. "Dishonorably discharged!" was Paderewski's final verdict against the League one evening after a long, discouraging discussion.

In 1940 Paderewski was named President of the National Council, which was the Polish government-in-exile. Together with President Raczkiewicz and General Sikorski, the three men were to operate wherever and however they could to keep alive the body and the spirit of Poland. But when France fell, Paderewski felt that he could do more if he could return to America. He was also sure that the United States could not remain much longer outside the conflagration that was sweeping across Europe.

In September Paderewski began his last (and what was to prove by far his most hectic) trip. His friends had been urging him for weeks to leave Switzerland as soon as possible. Great as his personal prestige and international reputation were, it was feared that, as the living spirit of exiled Poland, his life might be put in real danger at any moment. There were seven passengers in the two cars that left Riond-Bosson on September 23. One car was a Cadillac that Herbert Hoover had given Paderewski in Warsaw. The other one helped to carry the luggage of the party. At the Swiss-French border they were joined by an agent of the Sûreté Générale, the political police. Monsieur Garric had been assigned to the Paderewski party by the French Government to assist them in their journey, and he proved an invaluable addition before they were out of France. Time after time when the party was stopped for questions by various authorities, M. Garric merely flipped his lapel, revealing his badge, and the party continued on its way. And, of course, the name of Paderewski had the greatest possible effect. An official in the customs office at the Spanish border began to whistle the Minuet when he saw whose passports were passing over his desk.

Saragossa in Spain is the city that will go down in history as the only place ever to put Paderewski in prison. The President's entire party was placed under house arrest, and the fact that they were allowed to stay in their hotel did little to relieve the affront.

For five days, under a flimsy pretext of being con-

"*. . . to remain until Poland is free.*"

cerned for Paderewski's safety, the authorities of Saragossa kept the seven unwilling visitors confined to their hotel. Finally a cable from President Franklin Roosevelt direct to Generalissimo Franco got them out. No apology, no further explanation was ever heard from Saragossa. But by October, after a happy and reasonably relaxed trip through Portugal, they all boarded the American Export liner *Excambion*, and on November 6 they sailed into New York harbor. It was Paderewski's 80th birthday.

The Americans, who had loved and admired Paderewski for almost half a century, would have worn him out with receptions and dinners in his honor. But settling himself quietly in the Buckingham Hotel, he spent his time and strength in talking and corresponding with those who were most important to the present and future welfare of Poland. In June he asked to speak at a Polish war veterans' rally in Oak Ridge, New Jersey. The day was hot and the rally itself was a steamy, exhausting affair. Paderewski went home very tired and feeling as though he had caught a cold. Within a week, on the 29th of June, several hours after a priest had given him the sacrament of Extreme Unction, Paderewski died.

At his funeral in St. Patrick's Cathedral, with nearly 5,000 crowded inside and 35,000 outside lining Fifth Avenue and the adjacent streets, Cardinal, then Archbishop, Spellman eulogized Paderewski, saying "his death steeps the entire civilized world in mourning." And then the train took his body to Washington where it lay in state in the Polish Embassy until the following day.

The President of the United States had personally arranged for Paderewski's burial in a way that offered the greatest honor in the country's power. By special order, the body was taken to Arlington Cemetery, ordinarily reserved for American citizens who have served in their country's armed forces. As Paderewski's coffin, mounted on a military caisson, entered the gates of Arlington, cannon fired a 19-gun salute, the highest number possible to anyone not the head of a state. Flanked by United States soldiers, sailors, and marines, and joined by a squad of Polish soldiers in Canadian uniform, the caisson moved to the very center of the Cemetery. There, under the mast of the battleship *Maine*, Paderewski's coffin was placed in a vault "to remain until Poland is free."

The world is indebted to Paderewski in a very special way. To it he brought a flaming vision of great music-making. He placed before his listeners in singular glory the music of Chopin, one of the greatest composers of piano music the world has ever known. He carried to corners of the earth some of the most powerful pianism ever to be heard, never deviating from his own highest standards of excellence. Then, when his country's very existence was at stake, he proved himself an equal or even, in the opinion of some, a greater master in the arena of international politics. His genius extended to the devious ways of statecraft with the same penetration it had shown in the mastering of music's subtlest arts. His ability to influence men was as forceful when he spoke as it had been when channeled through the keys of a Steinway concert grand. He was unique in his lifetime. Nor has he had a successor.

INDEX

Alexander II, 13
Alma-Tadema, Laurence, 112
American Relief Administration, 149–151
Arlington Cemetery, 181

Balfour, Arthur, 144–145
Beethoven, Ludwig van
   "Appassionata" Sonata, 81
   C minor Piano Sonata, Opus 111, 136–137
   "Emperor" Concerto, 75
   "Moonlight" Sonata, 175
   Thirty-two Variations in C minor, 58
Brahms, Johannes, 49
Bryan, William Jennings, 91
Burne-Jones, Edward, 69–70

Carnegie Hall, 72, 74, 79, 134, 141, 164–167
Chopin, Frederic, 28, 58, 98, 101–102, 120, 127, 134, 136, 175, 182
Clemenceau, Georges, 123, 155–156, 166–167

Colonne, Edouard, 58, 60
Cooper, chef, 88
Cortot, Alfred, 59
Czerny studies, 53

Damrosch, Walter, 75
Daniels, Josephus, 139
Dmowski, Roman, 111, 144–145, 148, 153–155
Downes, Olin, 174
Dresden Opera, 98

Essipoff, Annette, wife of Leschetizky, 44

Fourteen Points, 141
Franz Ferdinand, Archduke, 105

Galli-Curci, Amelita, 83
Ganz, Rudolph, 106
George, Lloyd, 111, 153–154, 156
Germany, offer of Polish freedom, 128, 130
Gibson, Charles Dana, 166–167
Goerlitz, Hugo, 76, 89, 91, 93

Gorska, Helena, *see* Paderewska, Mme.
Gorski, Ladislas, 41–42
Gounod, Charles, 57
Grieg Concerto in A minor, 37
Grünwald, Battle of, 16–17, 101

Hitler, Adolf, 172, 176
Hofmann, Josef, 106
Hoover, Herbert, 91–93, 151, 178
House, Colonel Edward Mandell, 121–126, 129, 132, 134–135, 137, 141, 146, 156

Ignatius Loyola, St., 104–105

Kellogg, Vernon, 150
Kerntopf, Edward, 20–22, 26, 30, 55, 64, 86
Kontski, Apollinaire de, 19, 23, 29–30, 36
Korsak, Antonina, Paderewski's first wife, 39–41

Lamoureux, Charles, 58, 60
Lamoureux Orchestra, 60–61, 75

Lansing, Robert, 113–115, 131, 159
League of Nations, 177
Leschetizky, Theodore, 44, 46, 49, 51–56, 93
Liszt, Franz, 31, 59, 136, 175
  Hungarian Fantasia, 75
Loesser, Arthur, 84
Lucca, Pauline, 55

Madison Square Garden, 79, 170, 175
Massenet, Jules, 57
Mayer, Daniel, 65–66, 68
Mendelssohn, Felix, 136
Metropolitan Opera House, 99, 164, 166–167
Modjeska, Helen, 46–48
"Moonlight Sonata" (film), 172

Nicholas II, 109

Paderewska, Antonina, 15, 28, 86–87, 106, 111
Paderewska, Mme. Helena, 63, 95, 97, 99, 116, 124, 161, 170, 173
Paderewski, Alfred, 39–40, 62–63, 86, 97–98
Paderewski, compositions of,
  "Manru," 87, 98–99

Paderewski, compositions of (*cont.*)
Minuet in G, 94, 175, 178
Piano Sonata, Opus 21, 136
Symphony, 102
Variations in A minor, 44
Paderewski, Jan, 12–13, 16–22, 34–37, 86–87
Paris Peace Conference, 146, 152–153, 155
Pilsudski, Józef, 144–153, 159–160
Pius XI, Pope (Achille Ratti), 97–98
Poland, early achievements of, 118
Poland, partitions of, 13–14, 171
Polish army, 139–140
Polish Falcons, Union of, 139
Polish Relief Committee, 112
Pullman, Paderewski's private, 87–89, 168

Riond-Bosson, 97, 105–106, 110–111, 176, 178
Roosevelt, Franklin D., 139, 180–181
Rubinstein, Anton, 44–45, 70

Concerto in D minor, 77
Rubinstein, Artur, 45
Russia, offer of Polish freedom, 110
Russia, Paderewski tours of, 31–35, 96–97

Saint-Saens, Camille, 57, 69
Concerto in C minor, 61, 74
Salle Erard, 57, 59, 63
Samaroff, Olga, 106
San Francisco Exposition, 116
Schelling, Ernest, 106–108
Schoenberg, Arnold, 106
Schumann, Robert, 75, 136–137
Concerto in A minor, 75
Sienkiewicz, Henry, 111
Sigismond III, statue of, 27, 142
Sobieski, King John, 27
Spellman, Francis Cardinal, 181
Steinway and Sons, 71, 73, 78
Steinway, William, 74, 78–79, 82
Stojowski, Sigismond, 136
St. Patrick's Cathedral, 181
Strasbourg Conservatory, 54–55
Strauss, Johann, 49
Strauss, Richard, 40–41

Thibaud, Jacques, 165
Tretbar, Charles, 73–74, 78–79
Truman, Harry S, 96
Tchaikowsky, Peter, 57

Versailles, Treaty of, 157
Victoria, Queen, 71

Warsaw Conservatory, 17–19, 21–24, 29, 35, 38
Wilson, Woodrow, 122, 126–128, 131–133, 137–138, 141, 156, 177
Wooley, Robert, 124–125
Zamek, 27, 142, 151

The following is a list of some of the sources used by the authors in their research.

Paderewski and His Art, by Henry T. Finck. Wittingham, 1895.

America and the New Poland, by H. H. Fisher. The Macmillan Co., 1928.

"Paderewski, the Paradox of Europe," by Edward Mandell House. Harper's Magazine, 1925.

What Really Happened at Paris, edited by Col. Edward M. House and Charles Seymour. Charles Scribner's Sons, 1921.

Paderewski, by Charlotte Kellogg. The Viking Press, Inc., 1956.

Herbert Hoover, The Man and His Work, by Vernon Kellogg. D. Appleton Co., 1920.

Ignace Paderewski, by Rom Landau. Thomas Y. Crowell Co., 1934.

Pilsudski and Poland, by Rom Landau. The Dial Press, Inc., 1929.

War Memoirs of Robert Lansing. The Bobbs-Merrill Co., Inc., 1935.

The Paderewski Memoirs, by Ignace Jan Paderewski, with Mary Lawton. Charles Scribner's Sons, 1938.

Paderewski, The Story of a Modern Immortal, by Charles Phillips. The Macmillan Co., 1933.

Paderewski As I Knew Him, by Aniela Strakacz. Rutgers University Press, 1934.

THE AUTHORS AND THEIR BOOK

RUTH FOX HUME *was born in New York City and attended the College of New Rochelle. She attended medical school briefly, where she discovered that she was more interested in the history of medicine than in its practice. The result was* Great Men of Medicine *and* Milestones of Medicine. *While she pursued her writing career, she taught at Holy Cross Academy and Catholic University. Some recent books include* Our Lady Came to Fatima, Saint Margaret Mary *and* Florence Nightingale. *Mrs. Hume also writes book reviews for the* Washington Evening Star.

PAUL HUME *was born in Chicago and received a degree in music from the University of Chicago. He became music director of a "good music" radio station and then music critic of the Washington Post, a position he has held for sixteen years. He is a Professor of Music at Georgetown University and has been the director of the Georgetown Glee Club for twelve years. He is the author of* Catholic Church Music, *as well as many articles that have appeared in* The Saturday Review, The Sign, The Catholic Digest, *and others.*

THE LION OF POLAND *is the first book on which the Humes have collaborated. They live in Washington, D.C., with their four children, Paul, Michael, Ann and Peter.*

THE LION OF POLAND (*Hawthorn, 1962*) *was designed by Stefan Salter and completely manufactured by American Book–Stratford Press, Inc. The body type is Linotype Janson, based on the letters of Anton Janson, a Dutch punchcutter who worked between 1660 and 1687.*

A HAWTHORN BOOK

ABOUT CREDO BOOKS

CREDO BOOKS is an important new series of biographies that will appeal to both boys and girls. The subjects of these biographies are Catholic, but their stories are not of their faith so much as how that faith helped them to lead remarkable lives. Past and present will be represented here: a sculptor who left a priceless treasure of art to mankind, or a baseball player who has become an idol to young fans the world over; a movie star who was an idol of a different kind to young and old alike; the president of a South American country who fought against and lost his life to Communist terrorists. Heroes are made by the greatness of the human spirit and all the figures to be portrayed in CREDO BOOKS were great in spirit, courage and effort, no matter what task they took upon themselves.

The authors of these new books have been carefully chosen both for their ability to make biography come alive for young people and their knowledge of their subjects. Such authors as Hugh Ross Williamson, Lon Tinkle, Donald Demarest, Eva K. Betz, Ruth Hume, Frank Kolars and Jack Steffan will be represented.

To give CREDO BOOKS the benefit of their knowledge and experience, an editorial board of distinguished representatives from the fields of education, librarianship and the Catholic press, as well as Hawthorn's own editorial staff, choose both subject and author for each book in the series.

As an example of the variety of personalities in this new series, you will find the following figures portrayed.

Father Hugh O'Flaherty, by Daniel Madden
Francis X. Ford, by Eva K. Betz
Joyce Kilmer, by Norah Smaridge
Gary Cooper, by Richard Gehman
Thomas More, by Margaret Stanley-Wrench
Gregor Mendel, by Gary Webster
Michelangelo, by Anne M. Peck with Frank and Dorothy
  Getlein
Castillo Armas, by Jack Steffan
Ramon Magsaysay, by Gen. Carlos Romulo
Mother Katharine Drexel, by Katherine Burton
Tom Dooley, by Terry Morris
Juan Diego and the Virgin of Guadalupe, by Lon Tinkle
Mary, Queen of Scots, by Hugh Ross Williamson
Fra Junipero Serra, by Donald Demarest
Charlemagne, by Col. T. N. Dupuy
Pedro Menendez, by Frank Kolars

There is adventure, suspense, excitement and information in CREDO BOOKS.